New World Kids

The Parents' Guide
to Creative Thinking

New World Kids

Susan Marcus
Susie Monday

Austin • 2008

ISBN: 978-0-615-19060-0

New World Kids is a registered trademark of FoundryMedia

Designed by Susan Marcus
Most photographs by Allison V. Smith (details, back page)

Austin, Texas

This book is dedicated with love and gratitude to
Jearnine Wagner and Paul Baker for their lifetimes of
creativity, courage and commitment to the belief that
all children are born with creative genius.

Contents

Foreword

We need all the children now.

We need them to be aware of the abilities they bring to the world. And we need them to have the understandings to be confident and creative with those abillities.

This book is grounded in the belief that we are in the process of birthing a new world, and the landscape of meaning is shifting beneath our feet. There is a growing coherence around the knowing that the earth truly is a community and that we all share a common destiny. When we ponder that understanding we know, as parents, the skills and tools we now expect schools to give our children are no longer enough. They need more to cope and thrive in this new environment of change in which they are growing up.

We are now witnessing seismic shifts in the ways many institutions think and work. But the institution of education is one of the most resistant to change. Much of the curricula — even the ways intelligence is defined — are out of date. We believe that parents are the ones who can get ahead of this curve. Parents can not only demand change in schools for their children, but more importantly, *be* the change their children need now.

One important aspect of this educational shift is for parents to understand, value and teach *creative thinking* — at home, in the context of everyday. We have new understanding about how early children form their ideas about the how the world works, what's important and what's valued by the adults in their lives. Neuroscience, as well the fields of psychology, cognitive science and metacognition, support this understanding. Parents lay out (though not always consciously) the blueprint of values, habits and attitudes their children live by. It is through their parents' eyes that children get their first indelible impressions of themselves. And so, as parents, it's time to enlarge our own sense of what's important, what's to be valued and practiced.

It is our aim as educators, researchers and parents ourselves, to open this conversation. We've put together "New World Kids" as a handbook on creative thinking, a kind of "creativity 101." It is designed to respond to parents' need for the day-to-day, nuts-and-bolts ideas for activities that support the more conceptual beliefs they want to impart.

"New World Kids" has three main ingredients:

1. **The Sensory Alphabet** – a fresh look at the fundamentals children will need to undergird all the media they will be working with in the future — not just the skills related to words and numbers that form the "3 R's" of literacy today.

2. **A Map of Creativity** — a way of looking at different aspects of creativity and getting mental arms around a very big subject.

3. **Activities** — scattered throughout, that help parents get started thinking, watching, planning, designing and having fun with their children along the way. Activities are where the "rubber meets the road."

This book has grown out of decades of applied research with children, examining creativity, media, cognition and individuality. This was our work at the Learning About Learning Educational Foundation, a future-oriented research and development institution in Texas. Over the years (1968 – 1985), we worked with children, parents, teachers, schools and educators of all kinds; created programs and materials for local, national and global markets; and ran an influential Lab School. All our inquiries were based on the assumption that each of us has abundant, powerful and unique resources – all of us have creative potential – and that we are all mutually dependent on each other's creativity and productivity.

These beliefs and concerns have not changed.

Susan Marcus
Austin, Texas
October 2008

Introduction

Introduction

*The new conditions demand
a new way of thinking.
The new thinking demands
new forms of expression.
The new expression generates
new conditions.*

- Bruce Mau

Kids and the Future

We all want the best for our kids. We want to see them grow and bloom and become successful adults in the world. But when you look at your 2-year-old (or 5 or 10-year-old) today, it's hard to imagine what the world will be like or what their career choices will be by the time they're grown.

Global positioning devices, instant messaging, satellite phones on mountain tops, non-invasive surgery, networked terrorism, 'service' economies, even personalized jeans — all are indications of fundamental shifts in the ways we engage with the world and each other. Taken all together, it adds up to "the new world," a phrase that was first coined in the 15th century and has recently re-entered the popular lexicon. Whatever our various perspectives, we all now have a sense of what it means.

The scale of change, largely driven and enabled by technology, is unprecedented in human history. What's happening resembles the way a kaleidoscope works, with new connections happening between fields or thought processes or even countries. New ideas emerge and create new ripples of thinking; suddenly, a new pattern becomes visible, and a new picture falls into place.

It is the change itself, this re-ordering, this inventing "the new world" that will occupy our children's future. We are entering a time that will call for dedicated innovation across the board. It will occur in all fields; in fact it has already started. But unfortunately, where our kids are concerned, what we're teaching is "business as usual."

4

Ironically, business has been writing about the future for a decade now, ruminating about the rapid unfolding of technology, the interdependencies of globalization, the acceleration of change and what is needed to cope with it. All this analyzing and strategizing has produced a best-selling stash of books and magazines about the future. And what they say we need is *innovation*.

So where does innovation start? Why aren't we considering this in relation to kids? *They are* the future, after all. And while we're still measuring *"how"* we teach instead of *"what"* we teach, kids are out there, moving at light speed, adapting, and living deeply in the world their senses report as true. So far, we haven't offered much help.

Critical and Creative Thinking

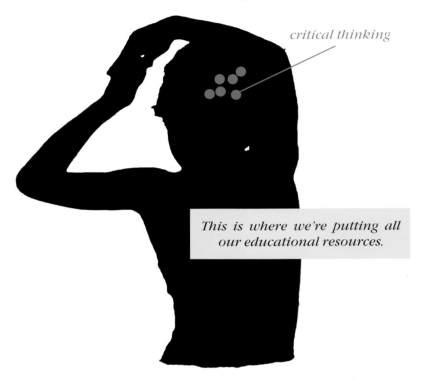

There's a big gap between how our kids need to be equipped to deal with the future and how we're preparing them now. The standards we use were developed to cope with the rise of the Industrial Revolution a century and a half ago. Designed for the "new" public education, they were just what was needed then. It's where children learned the basic literacies of our culture related to words and numbers. This is still the case. Our standardized tests reflect this.

The thinking skills that are taught and applied generally fall under the umbrella of what are now called critical thinking skills, associated with analyzing and weighing information. These skills and literacies are very important to learn, but

*This is where kids are really **living**.*

they are no longer enough. The institution of education hasn't yet caught up with what children need to learn now and for the future.

Kids naturally gravitate into the daily world of sounds, layered images and simultaneous events. This sensory world is up close, technological, connected, visually rich, emotional and immediate. It's about friends, fun, computers, games, stories, animals, cell phones, TV, wonders, worries, playing, communicating, family, music and sports.

It's where pop culture lives. It's also where the senses and the imagination live...*outside the box.*

It's time to rethink — to incorporate, teach and *value* the kinds of thinking that are closer to the "creative" end of the thinking spectrum. That's a challenge for our culture, which often views creativity with suspicion. Although we admire shining examples of creative achievement, we tend to believe it's a mysterious process. Or another magical matter of *talent*. And besides, it's hard to measure.

But the standard 3-R's won't take us where we need to go. The facts, figures and unconnected blueprints of subjects that make up school curricula create what is like a still image in a world that is instead liquid and changing.

creative thinking

critical thinking

It is only in the rich and somewhat unpredictable tumble of a valued child and his or her individual mix of data and magic that we can hope for a healthy, thriving planet.

8

Along with traditional thinking skills, it's now essential to add: many media, creating, making connections, approaching a subject sideways, or solving a problem from the inside out — in other words, the kind of thinking fluent enough to come up with the innovations the future will demand. It's about learning a sensory vocabulary, perceiving larger patterns and jumping mental fences. It's also about allowing intuition, putting your hands in and applying your unique fingerprints.

It's Where Innovation Begins

Innovation is often understood as bringing new methods, products or ideas into a field or industry that has already been established. It assumes a familiarity with the information and processes that exist. It's a new step forward — it might be a baby step or a giant leap. But it's a grown-up idea.

The child's counterpart to innovation is *creative thinking*. Practicing creative thinking can hone the natural tendencies we see so often in children's play into a firm foundation of thinking skills that will serve them (and us) in the future.

It's not a matter of chance or talent or luck, creative thinking is a matter of focus and practice. Like reading, it's a skill that is learned by doing. Inborn imagination and natural creativity become fluent thinking tools when children learn to see patterns, use associative thinking and practice creating. Also, just like reading, adults help kids along by supplying the right challenge at the right time.

Consider reading. It's a skill built on the foundation of several diverse elements: you have to know the squiggles that make up the alphabet and the sounds associated with those abstract symbols, how words are constructed out of them, the way to move your eye down the line of letters to come up with the sounds that make the words like spoken words. You build these sensibilities a little at a time. Somewhere along the way, meanings start to pop into your brain — and you're reading! You get better at it as you go along.

Creative thinking (as a skill) works the same way. It's grounded in diverse elements. It is enhanced by a sensory vocabulary (elemental building blocks, like the alphabet) and through experiences with a kind of thinking not necessarily involved with words — the kinds of knowings that your senses and your body are good at, like riding a bike, or judging relative weights or seeing your favorite color. Often some kind of media comes next — like pencils or cameras or drums — as a way for ideas to take form. Creative thinking (often in the presence of a problem to solve) consciously rubs these diverse elements together and (presto!) ideas and meanings start to pop into your brain.

Creative thinking is generative thing. It honors intuition but doesn't leave out analysis. It uses data, but also looks for larger patterns. It is flexible and fluent. It is the kind of thinking that is the foundation for innovation in all fields, from physics to engineering to cooking. And it is a sought-after quality in the current business environment.

This Is Where Parents Come In

The good news is that kids live and breathe this *creative thinking*. It's as basic as its more trusted counterpart, *critical thinking,* just less measurable. Humans come by it naturally; it's our heritage, our human nature. We just don't honor it. In fact, research tells us this kind of thinking is almost squeezed out of our kids by fourth grade. This is where parents play a crucial role. We all want to see our kids grow up happy and successful. But now the game is changing.

Success may rely on rethinking the "basics" and adding creative thinking to the list of skills that is practiced and applauded. Schools are focused elsewhere. It's up to parents to fill this gap. If parents don't give kids a strong foundation in creative thinking, they probably won't get it. If parents don't value it, kids won't. It's that simple. It's time to open this conversation about kids and future-oriented skills with parents. It's past time.

But for parents, it can be anxiety producing! At first glance, nurturing creative thinking in children can sound like a very large and ongoing agenda that won't fit into already tight schedules and overcrowded mental real estate. We hope to put your anxieties to rest and to assure you that nurturing creativity in your everyday life at home can be a real source of fun! It can generate energy instead of drain it. It can enlarge your child's idea of what success looks like. It can be an important window into your child's natural strengths. It will better prepare your child for the future. And, not least, it will make unique, memorable events for everyone to share.

Through our work with The Learning About Learning Educational Foundation and its nationally recognized lab school, we've gathered lots of knowledge and experience about this kind of thinking. This book is the result of 35 years of applied research into the nature of creativity, media, individuality and cognition. Just as important are the same number of years in work/play with educators, parents and kids, designing processes and projects, spaces and experiences.

And as parents, researchers and educators, ourselves, we've designed this handbook on creative thinking with parents' and caregivers' needs in mind. It's full of ideas, plans, tools and support. It can be an important resource for anyone who wants to activate his or her child's creative potential.

"New World Kids" is grounded in the belief that we are all mutually dependent on the diverse creative abilities and productivity of each other and that everyone possesses abundant, unique and powerful resources. The following goals emerge from this belief and inform our approach:

Goals for Raising
New World Kids

INITIATION

We want our children to take responsibility for helping to shape their everyday lives. We want to see them generating their own ideas and activities, rather than waiting passively to be entertained, bullied by peer pressure or engulfed by consumerism.

DIVERSITY

Each individual has a unique viewpoint from which to work and create. We want to nurture a curiosity about other people that grows from our child's understanding and confidence in his or her unique perspective.

RESPONSIVENESS

We want our children to be present and responsive to what's going on around them, neither tuning out nor acting out. We want to see engagement not boredom, energy not lethargy, focus not frenzy. We want them to pay attention.

SHARING

We want our family members to enjoy each other, working on each other's ideas, plans, interests and inventions. We want to take advantage of the power of the group. We want everyone in our family to initiate, plan and direct activities in which others can participate.

SUPPORT

Supporting each other's growth and development, we appreciate our differences and celebrate our varied strengths and talents. We want to help each other reach goals, solve problems and grow strong.

FLEXIBILITY

We want our children to reflect on their behaviors and habits, letting go of those that hold them back. In new situations, we want them to build new habits and develop positive and productive new behaviors.

PROBLEM SOLVING

When our children grapple with everyday problems, we want to see them generate not one, but dozens of possible solutions. If our child has only one way of relating to others — as the bully, as the clown, as the whiner — we want him or her to see beyond that role to other ways of communicating and negotiating. If our children are caught in negative situations, we want them to know how to change the situation, leave it or find its unexpected gifts.

RESOURCEFULNESS

Each of us has a universe of resources. We want to see our children making good use of time, energy, spaces, materials and experiences. We don't want to raise wasteful children.

CREATIVITY

We want our children to act creatively, to see each experience as an opportunity for invention, to be skilled at giving form to their ideas and at cultivating many options for communicating their ideas to other people.

Part 1:

Mapping Creativity

A Map of Creativity

It can be useful to look at creativity as the sum of various parts — parts that are not alike and don't necessarily form a sequence. One way to understand the different parts is to use the elements inherent in reading as an analogy: phonics, the left-to-right sweep of the eye across lines of type, the foundation of the alphabet. Each element is important yet distinct. The following chapters consider each part of creativity separately, defining, enlarging and giving you ideas about how to use it — both as a lens into your child's unique creative potential and as the basis of activities to grow creativity in the context of everyday.

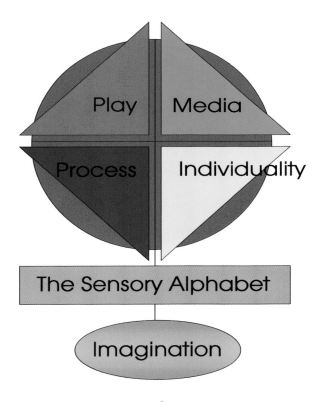

1. Imagination is a given. Everybody has one, and it's available 24/7. It constantly fuels little ideas, such as "What can I make for a snack?" and big dreams, like "What can I be when I grow up?" The more you feed your imagination with observations and experiences and memories, the richer and wiser your imagination becomes — and the more and better ideas it can give you.

2. The sensory alphabet is to creativity what the traditional alphabet is to reading. First, you learn it; then you can put its elements (like alphabet letters) to work in unlimited ways, seeing and making all sorts of new patterns. It's the same as being able to read or write any word you can think of after you learn your letters.

3. Media is anything you use to get your ideas from the inside of your brain out into the world. It might be *words* you say, or *chalk* to draw a game idea on the sidewalk, or a *costume* that helps you make a character for your drama idea. The more you play with all kinds of different media, the more it feeds your imagination.

4. Play is the heart of creativity. Play puts ideas in motion. Playing by yourself lets you see your ideas out in the world, which gives you more ideas. Playing with another person gives your ideas a chance to interact with others' ideas and multiplies them. Experts recognize that play is *thinking in action*, without the consequences of "the real world." This freedom is important for growing ideas.

5. Individuality is another given. But it can be hard to see yourself and how you're different and what your strengths are. This is where parents come in, watching with care, mirroring a child's strengths, providing media and experiences that match each child's unique brand of imagination — and supplying challenges that stretch each child's imagination. It turbo-charges individual creative potential.

6. The creative process isn't really mysterious, it's a particular way of thinking, like critical thinking or the scientific method. Kids start out doing it naturally and unconsciously. But when you learn and practice this way of thinking consciously, the results are dramatic. It's like adding reading and writing to your speaking skills. It's a thinking skill that can turn imagination into jet fuel for ideas, and for grown-up innovation later on.

The next chapters will expand on each element of creativity.

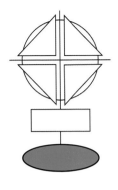

Imagination:
The Source

The possible's slow fuse is lit,
by the Imagination.

— Emily Dickinson

Imagination

The imagination is like a very deep well. And we don't know where the bottom of that well is exactly. Big ideas and little ideas surface in our imaginations all the time. We have clear indications where some ideas come from — maybe from logical thinking or certain expertise or memory. Other ideas pop up quite unexpectedly, "from left field" as the saying goes — maybe from a dream or a hunch.

When you factor in the notion that we think with all parts of our brain and body, you realize just how much we depend on our imaginations all the time. After all, it's your imagination that's giving you the kinetic idea of how to take a new shortcut to the grocery store, or the visual idea of which socks look "right" to wear today, or the spatial idea of where you parked in a vast parking lot, or the "feeling" that a recipe won't work because it's too "dry." Most of the work our imaginations do for us goes unnoticed and undervalued.

When we first come into the world as babies, the imagination is going full steam, a superhighway of intention to all the senses as we take in the blooming, buzzing confusion of our world — looking, tasting, smelling, touching, and opening every drawer that's remotely possible to open. Little by little, the imagination gets reined in by parents and caregivers who teach us to follow our cultural blueprint. We are shown when to sleep, what to eat, where to pee, what not to touch and how to use language. It's called growing up.

Play is the arena where the imagination still reigns. One of the kinds of thinking linked to the imagination is "divergent thinking." It is also one way of measuring creativity. Young children typically score very highly in divergent thinking.

But when school starts, we begin to shut the door on the imagination as we commence teaching and valuing the logical and linear thinking that supports reading and mathematics. This is called "convergent thinking." Then, early on, scores in "divergent thinking" begin to diminish significantly. This is not to say that we don't need the "convergent" skills that are associated with words and numbers, we just need to value and make time for and give attention to the skills related to all kinds of thinking.

Inborn individual differences in the ways we are wired, by genes and heredity, are also associated with the natural brand of imagination we have. If we are born athletes, we'll always have an easy connection to movement, and "kinetic ideas" will flow naturally. Likewise, with innately visually oriented people; their best ideas might be in colors, not words. A budding engineer's ideas will be spatial, with a clear "knowing" of what will fit and move and "work" to solve a problem. These differences are now generally called "multiple intelligences," a term coined by Howard Gardner in his groundbreaking research at Harvard. We each have some unique mixture of them. (See more on this in the "Individuality" chapter.)

We need to keep our imaginations filled up and flowing by feeding and exercising them. That means having experiences of all kinds, using all the senses and exercising the imagination with play. Remember, the imagination is not necessarily partial to words. It loves all sorts of media. Experiment with making bread dough, building a tower with marshmallows and straws, balancing on a board, making a light show with gels and flashlights, designing a treehouse. Do this on a regular basis. You may not remember your experiments the next week, but your imagination will, and be richer and deeper and able to give you more ideas.

Here is a specific way to build imagination and "ideational fluency":

The Junk Jar

This is an activity that relies on associative thinking. It can be done by one person alone, or with the whole family as an after-dinner game. Fill a big empty gallon jar with tidbits that you find interesting for one reason or another: a feather, shells, old coins, a ribbon, a rock, twigs, buttons, a pinecone....

Each person chooses one object for to use as his or her prompt. Notice the diversity of the minds around your dining room table through their choices. We predict you'll be surprised by the different paths taken, and by the similarities and differences that will show up in the end.

• Observe the one thing.

• Make a list of adjectives that describe your object. Take 10 or 15 minutes to let your mind wander. Consider it as a historian would, a scientist, a painter, a choreographer, a mapmaker, a sculptor. Feel free to add more viewpoints.

• Answer these questions: If this object were a time of day, what would that be? If it were a season, what would it be? Weather?

• Then, looking over your whole list of qualities... what kind of person could those qualities describe? How old would this person be? What would he look like? What would she be wearing? Name him/her.

Give this person some history. Think about how this person could have gained the qualities you've written down. Write and draw.

• After that, decide what is your character's biggest concern.

Now you've used associative thinking to take you from an object to a full-fledged character. Something from your imagination. If more than one person has been participating, take your creations even further. First, share what you've created. Then, let your characters interact. Give them a problem to solve. Make a story line. You might even decide to write and illustrate it or make a video. Let your ideas grow and germinate in your imagination. Record ideas that come to you over the next few days. You'll be surprised at what your imagination will come up with.

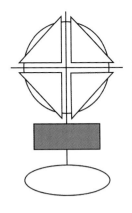

The Sensory
Alphabet:
the Foundation

*There are children playing in the street
who could solve my top problems
in physics because they have
modes of sensory perception
that I lost long ago.*

— J. Robert Oppenheimer

How Do You See Beyond the Obvious?

Our brains work so quickly and efficiently to construct meaning around our perceptions of the world that often we don't notice the elemental qualities of our experience. We immediately and unconsciously leap right into defining, labeling and judging. We don't see the bowl of yellow shapes, we see *lemons.* We don't see the green prickly lines on a tree, we see *pine needles.* We don't hear the rhythm that makes Texans want to dance, we hear the *two-step.*

And so, from babyhood on, we are off on our lifelong journey of naming, labeling and pigeonholing the world around us. It's the perceptual shorthand we need and use so that we don't have to focus on every little thing. It is also the textbook for thinking *inside* the box.

But when our goal is nurturing creativity, we begin with a more elemental approach. The Sensory Alphabet, which follows, is in essence a sensory language — a different way of describing what our senses are telling us is out there. It focuses on the patterns that underlie what we experience. By naming this vocabulary, it allows us to give voice to what we perceive in ways unburdened by the boundaries, definitions or prejudices of our culture. It opens up our perceptions for analysis, comparison, designing and creating. It builds curiosity and generates ideas.

When children absorb and use this sensory vocabulary on an everyday basis, it becomes second nature. It is easy for them to spot the elements. They're close at hand, or eye, or ear. The elements feel welcome to a young mind that's been taught so early the highly abstract forms of the alphabet and

26

numbers, as those in our culture do. Every child can master this vocabulary of sensing, comparing and contrasting. It offers a hands-on, eyes-on, all-senses-on path of discovery and delight. And it is in direct contrast to the often visually hypnotic, passive and repetitive qualities of television and video games. It's the natural foundation for deep interaction with the world.

Because this sensory vocabulary describes, but doesn't define, it enlarges the capacity for seeing patterns between disparate objects, fields and cultures. This ability to perceive patterns is one of the hallmarks of a creative mind.

The DNA of "Stuff"

The Sensory Alphabet is a set of attributes elemental to our planet. It's how our senses report to our brains what is *out there*. It's how we can describe anything and everything. You could say it makes up the DNA of "stuff."

There are nine elements: **line, shape, color, texture, sound, space, light, movement and rhythm.** These elements are givens. And though they are familiar, most of us don't explore their powers or use them consciously for problem solving and creating.

Often we think of these elements as belonging to the territory of the arts or design, and, of course, they are potent tools for those fields. But if we step back from our usual definitions, it's easy to see how these elements underlie all our perceptions. **Rhythm**, for example, belongs not only to music but is also basic information to a doctor assessing an electrocardiogram. **Rhythm** is at the heart of devising a spectacular basketball play, a winning debate, or creating a dramatic cinematic moment in the film editing room.

Another example: we might first think of **space** as the tool and consideration of architects, but it's also what tickles the imaginations of physicists and graphic designers — and it's very important when you're parallel parking. The examples are endless. These are the elements that make up the patterns our senses take in and to which our brains, instantly and unconsciously assign meaning and value. When a pattern of qualities — say, **shape** and **color** and **texture** — resonates in a certain way, we recognize a dog or a tree or a vase.

Some patterns have become emblematic of our culture: the **rhythms** of rock and roll, the amount of conversational **space** between people that can be identified as distinctly western, or the series of **lines** we have come to know as our alphabet. We share these essences and meanings with others in our culture, and when we travel we are often surprised at how other cultures have combined these elements quite differently. Even though the essences and meanings are similar, the accepted closer conversational **space** of another culture might, to us, feel threatening, too "in your face." Standard cultural **colors** in another region might feel drab to us, or conversely, too bright.

At a more granular, individual level there seems to be a built-in sense of what is comfortable when it comes to these elements — certain preferences that come out so early they seem to be inborn. Every parent who has more than one child can attest to this.

We all have favorites — certain qualities of **light** or **rhythm** —

that are distinctively different from the preferences of other members of our family, certain kinds of **sounds** that are appealing, or a sense of **space** that is "just right" to each person.

These preferences are often expressed unconsciously in the choices an individual makes — for instance, by dressing in favorite colors, by demonstrating a love of texture with hairstyles or through jewelry or by using big movements and gestures again and again.

In this country we teach young children these elements somewhat haphazardly, quickly jumping to the labels and meanings our culture has assigned: **shapes** are *squares* or *circles*, sounds are *"what the cow says"* or just *"too loud."* Rhythm is usually defined by music. We seldom explore **shape** for its own sake, or **sound**, or **rhythm**. But as researchers, educators and parents, we have observed that these elements, explored individually and absorbed slowly and deeply over time, can become a potent sensory vocabulary of understandings for children.

A Symbol System for the Senses

Another way to think about the Sensory Alphabet is as a *symbol system* — a set of symbols that we can use to communicate information.

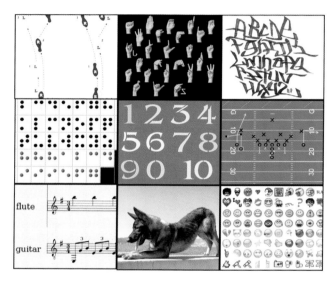

Above are several of the sysmbol systems that we use in this culture. You are probably familiar with them, some more intimately than others. Clockwise from the upper left:

1. These lines and shapes that are notations for a dance; in this case, the tango.
2. These are the gestures that comprise American Sign Language.
3. These lines make up our alphabet.
4. These lines describe football plays.
5. These are shapes and lines meant to communicate emotions — "emoticons."
6. If you're lucky enough to speak "dog," you'll know that this gesture (one of many) is asking you to play.
7. These dots and lines signify sounds and pacing (music!).

8. The dots here are raised, and therefore have texture.
   This is Braille, another way of making the alphabet.
9. These lines are numbers, symbolizing amounts.

When you look at these symbol systems at their most elemental level, you'll see lines and shapes, colors and movement (gestures). Long ago, we assigned them meanings, and today we teach these symbol systems to the next generation along with the skills for using them to communicate meaning.

We currently teach two symbol systems at school. They are, of course, letters (or the alphabet) and numbers. We base the skills we teach, test and value now on those systems — and we call them verbal literacy and numerancy.

Symbol System	Media	Expressive Forms
traditional alphabet	Spoken words (language)	Oratory, singing, conversations, etc.
	Written Words (reading and writing)	Contracts, books, email, grocery lists, reports, etc.
Numbers	Mathematics (algebra, arithmetic, geometry, etc.)	Cosmology, accounting, clocks, scorekeeping, bank statements, physics, etc.

But, as parents, the Sensory Alphabet is another symbol system that you'll want your kids to know and be literate with. It is the foundation for much of the digital media that are the predominate media of our children's future. Just think of the photos, music, iconography and video that are such a big part of most kids' daily lives.

Adults have a tendency to equate the ease with which their children manipulate digital media with real thinking skills based in the content that is delivered by that media. But this is not the case. The new literacies of the future include the thinking skills and the creativity that can grow out of this sensory symbol system.

Symbol System	Media	Expressive Forms
sensory alphabet	Cameras, paint, fabric, food, clay, computers, animals, pencils, paper, etc. ...STUFF	Cooking, gardening, carpentry, dancing, teaching, business, engineering, etc... EVERYTHING ELSE

What we need to add now.

The following pages introduce the Sensory Alphabet briefly, an overview of the elements and where we find them in our daily lives. Later, we give you ways to put these building blocks together.

The Sensory Alphabet

Color

Human vision is distinguished by the color-detecting ability of our eyes. For us, color is often the element of discernment — and the visual language of emotion.

Green with envy, seeing red, walking around under a black cloud — emotion transforms itself into colorful characters, colorful language, poetic passion. Paint on canvas creates sunny weather or an emotional storm; and color in music paints a picture solemn or spritely. Where is *your* color sense alive? In cooking or chemistry, stargazing or paint mixing, finding rainbows, delighting in a feather's iridescence or in an outlandishly fabulous fashion sense?

Sound

Sound has the inherent quality of acting directly on the emotions without going through the intellect.

Listen. The world is speaking to you in 1,000 different voices. When we listen, we put ourselves in the moment: present to an argument, a plea, a whine, a bird call, wind in the trees or a symphony. Besides the obvious (musicians and music), actors, politicians, priests and parents invoke action with tone, timber, tempo and sound. Writers (and readers) listen as words unfurl on the page. Painters may paint a sound and runners may use one to make the miles fly. Ecologists, anthropologists, birdwatchers, linguists and physicians all use sound to diagnose, distinguish and define.

Light

Light delights as the most elusive and changeable element of form: giving contour, creating mood, illuminating all manners of truth.

The sea sparkles, pearls have luster, silk shimmers, we "see the light." Stage designers, cinematographers, photographers and architects are obvious masters of light and shadow. But think, too, about light as perceived by physicists, glass artists, poets and urban planners. Without light, we're literally and figuratively "in the dark." Fireflies, fireworks, shadow play and starlight are some of our first light-filled fascinations – what are others?

Space

Space is omni-dimensional, geographic and temporal, both geometrically present outside of us and metaphorically present inside the fences of our imaginations.

With space, what *isn't* is as important as what *is:* the inside of a basket, the silences between the notes, the pause between the speakers, the room inside the walls. A canvas' size or a room's dimensions determine how we move within it. As humans, we can't help but pay attention to space as space and space as time. How long? How wide? How fast? How slow? Where and when? Think about how these people use and analyze space: mechanical engineers, publishers, architects, dancers, cartographers, chess players, editors, sitcom writers.

Movement

Movement is about change and getting from here to there, from up to down, from then to now.
We talk about how ideas move us, how ambition drives us, how responsibility keeps us tied down, how our imaginations run away and our philosophies collide. A story line must move right along or it loses our attention; cycles of days and years and viewpoints become the stuff of history; cycles in our bodies, in weather and in nature present whole worlds of study. Kinesthetic learners must move into knowledge, often quite literally, finding the meaning of a concept by physically moving into it. Movers include (but are not limited to) explorers, botanists, meteorologists, dancers, acrobats, athletes, construction workers, industrial designers.

Rhythm

Rhythm is the heartbeat element, holding things together in big and little patterns.

We each have a personal rhythm as distinct as our fingerprints, recognizable beneath the changing tides of emotional rhythms that rock and roll us through the day. Rhythm at first thought is audible and invisible — drum beats, finger taps, cadences and cacaphony — but imagine the world without stripes, dots and dashes, without the visual patterns of steps, of lines of shoes, of the this and that way of the lines in a leaf. Without rhythm, who could be a pianist, a mathematician, a poet, an actor, a director, a salesman, a video editor, a debater, a basketball player, a waiter, a politician, an animal behaviorist or a juggler?

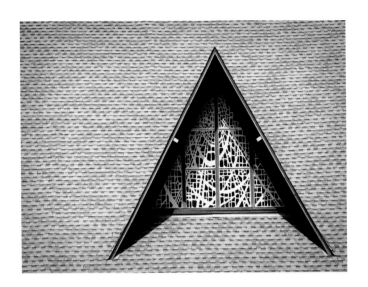

Line

Line, the elemental foundation for print and number, has determined much about 20th century life and success in our culture.

Isobars, arteries, fault lines, line drives, battle lines, lines of credit, timelines, lines of type, notes, numbers and people — stretchy, slinky, fixed or floating, dotted or dashed, lines connect two or more points. And the points are, as mathematicians remind us, infinite. Writers pen story lines; programmers, lines of code. Biologists decipher lines of DNA; entrepreneurs develop product lines. Singers follow melodic lines; jazz musicians improvise upon them. Where do you enter the element of line? As story teller or scribbler? With delight for a maze or an appreciation for ballet?

Shape

"Shapes shape other shapes." As shape finders we look for symmetries, for foreground and background, the doughnut and the hole, for the whole of the thing that is greater than its parts.

Putting puzzles together is playing around with shape and so is the literary love of beginning, middle and end. Pleasing shapes play their part in our neighborhoods, our furniture, our plates, platters, shoes and cars. Shapemakers include sculptors and typographers, mathematicians with their worlds of symmetries, microbiologists, industrial designers and couture clothiers. We shape play with shells and rocks, clay and cookie dough, big bouncing balls and smooth, sleek kitty cats.

Texture

At its most direct, tactile information is as close as it gets, up close and personal, right at our fingertips.
Smooth, woven, wrapped, slippery, shiny, course, rigid and reedy. We see texture, too, and hear it in a voice or a song. Our days are rough or smooth, our moods even or edgy, our voices piercing or pointed. Surgeons, weavers, gardeners, art collectors, textile designers and chefs must all pay close attention to texture. Do you remember exploring texture in the sand box, through a microscope's lens, coiling clay snakes, eating ice cream or squishing toes in the mud?

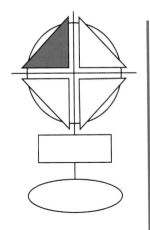

Play:
The Heart of
Creativity

Play is the brain's favorite way of learning.

— Diane Ackerman

Potent Play

Take play seriously! Little kids know that. And everyone knows that it's okay for them to play. But by the time kids enter grammar school, play begins to be a little tarnished and thought of as not so good. It can begin to mean "playing around," or "fooling around" or even "messing around." By the time kids are in middle school, the only kind of playing that seems okay is playing sports — or maybe playing a video or board game.

We all know the stories of burnt-out kids, children whose lives are structured morning to night with sports, art/piano/language/chess lessons, play dates, overnights and outings. In the very real life our kids live, it's all too easy to slide down the something-scheduled-every-afternoon slope. For one thing, with two active career parents, there's the after-school care quandary. In the city where many of us live, daydreaming space is at a premium. Raised on three-second sound bytes, MTV edits and razor-timed PlayStation modules, kids clamor for more and faster and often find the endless summer firefly kind of time boring.

But time for play — aimless, unstructured, "unproductive" — is important if you want to build a big imagination for creativity. It lets kids get some distance from everyday reality and deal with ideas instead of actual things and situations. In play, the accent is on creating, from creating characters to making forts, from doodling to climbing. Children can try out ideas, processes and perspectives that they couldn't or wouldn't in the real world. There are no consequences! They don't have to worry.

Experts know that *play is thinking in action*. Play gives kids a chance to rehearse, direct, invent, imitate, fantasize, try on, try out, experiment, rethink, rearrange, start over, express and explore...all very important for developing imaginative skills and fluency of ideas. Innovators consistently acknowledge the power of play in their own lives. As parents, we need to allow time for play in the increasingly busy lives of kids and to rejuvenate our own creative thinking as well. There are endless forms of play. Reacquaint yourself with five of them

1. Play with roles. Pretend.

Pretending lets us imitate something we've seen or read or thought about. It's like trying on an identity. Pretend to be a banker, for instance; try out a banker's thinking by lending "money," counting, evaluating risks and rewards. There's no worry about losing any real money! Or how about a detective? Or a rancher? It's a great time to experiment. Pretending to be a dancer, or a mommy with a new baby, or CEO of a new Internet company gives a child a sense of what it might be like. Stretch the imagination.

2. Role play with another person.

Adding one or more players stretches imaginations further. Partners in play have to cope with ideas and situations that another person dreams up. When kids play "house" or "pirate ship" the imagination holds up the roof or walks the plank. A version of this kind of activity for big kids might be to create a "play" with roles and jobs for several people: writing, directing, music, lighting, acting, set designing, video-taping, editing. This can be a powerful form of "play."

3. Play with materials.

Put your hands in. Joining hands to imaginations
makes an important connection. Kids will find
that as they play with different materials, the
materials start "talking back." They will start
having ideas about something else to try with a
different color, or texture, or shape...or, maybe if
they added a feather, then.... This kind of play can
start them down an interesting path of exploring
and creating.

4. Play in motion.

Get a move on. Stretching and strengthening muscles has its counterpoint in the mind. The over-and-over repetition involved in learning to skip rocks, pump a swing, bounce a ball or jump rope can foreshadow the kind of mastery that later is needed when commiting multiplication tables to memory, learning a dance or writing a business plan. Think of all the ways body language mirrors the qualities we want for an innovative mind: flexibility, strength, quickness, endurance, concentration.

5. Wild play. Play in the real world.

Humans evolved in a wild world. And while finding our way back to the wilderness may not be as easy as it was when just outside the door, children (and parents) instantly respond to even a little bit of "wild". Throwing dirt clods, skipping stones on a pond, watching an ant hill, wading in running water, lying back in the grass to watch the clouds change shapes — all these embody this quality of play. And no, the Disney-ish "nature" of theme parks really isn't the same. Even some city parks have wild corners, and if you live a suburban life, you might find a little bit of wild along your back fence.

49

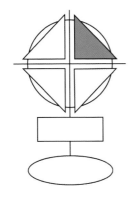

Media:
Bringing Ideas
into the World

My idea didn't work in paint,
so I tried it in clay.

— Joan, 10, LAL child

Media — It Matters

When you hear the word "media" today, it usually connotes some kind of journalism, either newspapers, magazines or television. Media used this way most often means "mass media," some form of information designed to reach many people at once.

But the original meaning of the word media comes from the same Latin word *media*, and it's the plural form of the word. The singular form is "medium"; two or more "mediums" make media. It originally meant "in between" or "the middle." The Latin phrase that's used sometimes in our legal documents, "in media res," means "in the middle of things."

In fact, the medium is in the middle of things. It's whatever material you use to make an idea apparent to the senses. If you're talking, the medium consists of spoken words that make your ideas apparent to someone else's ears. If you are giving directions to someone, the medium could be spoken words or written words. Or the medium might be drawn lines on a piece of paper: a map. A mathematical idea is expressed with numbers. You might make a chart of media that you use everyday to get your ideas across.

Idea	Medium	Form
Story of two brothers	Sung words	Opera
Story of two brothers	Spoken words	Play
Story of two brothers	Written words	Book
Pythagorean theorem	Numbers	Equation
New gossip	Written words	Texting
New gossip	Spoken words	Phoning
Directions to the zoo	Drawing	Map

You get the idea. You use many media every day to get your ideas and your messages across. And, as you can imagine, some media are better than others for the job. Take the problem of giving your friend directions to the zoo. You could give her verbal directions, telling her how to get there with spoken words. You might even use your hands to give her more information, showing how the road curves just a little to the right.

But you might want to write the directions down with words, noting the landmarks she'll pass on the way. Or you might give her a map, one that's been printed. The tiny lines and words on that map give lots of information about distance and direction. But you might be standing outside with nothing to work with and no map in your pocket, so you draw a map in the dirt with your finger. Your dirt map might be able to get a rough idea across, but you won't have the same amount or kind of information that the printed, colored lines have.

So, the important thing here is: the medium that expresses an idea or a message has a big effect on that information. It shapes the idea, emphasizing certain aspects, diminishing others. A medium can produce a strong impact, like a good ad. Or it can be faint, like a whisper in the wind. When you are choosing your medium of expression and are conscious of its possible effects, you're more in control. And the more media you are familiar with, the more ways you have to express your ideas. Common sense.

There's another interesting quality about media. When you really get into it, when you really give your attention to the medium you're using, it begins to talk back. It begins to give you ideas. Experts in any field would agree. As the carpenter works with wood, his imagination gains depth, and what he can create and predict about what is possible with wood grows. The same holds with cooks and food, physicists and numbers, clothing designers and fabrics. The list is infinite.

Common sense also tells us that we want our children to experience many media — pounding and shaping clay, beating drums and blowing whistles, singing and whispering, mixing paint and mixing batter, turning cartwheels and dancing, drawing with thin pen lines and also fat brushes, writing poems and writing essays, braiding hair and

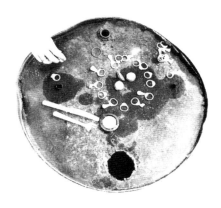

twisting rope, building with blocks and building with sand. Here are more media ideas: draw with water on the sidewalk, oil paint on boards, colored inks on tissue paper, icing on a cake, or chalk on the playground. Paint with sponges, sticks, rubber stamps, old toothbrushes. Sculpt with playdough, clay, twigs, paperclips, wood scraps. What would happen if you sewed together really big paper shapes with yarn and stuffed them with wadded up newspaper? Built a city out of milk cartons? A 30-foot creature out of sand at the beach? Filled up an empty room with strings and masking tape?

Playing and getting familiar with many media creates a deep well of resources for children to draw from. It fills the imagination (though not necessarily consciously) and gives them more ideas and more flexibility and power to communicate their ideas.

Parents are key here. If parents value and support a child's beginning work/play in various media — whether cooking, drawing with chalk on the sidewalk, or building a hamster house — the child will take away the sense that other things and other senses are valued along with those test scores.

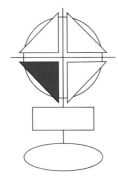

Creative Thinking: The Process

Creativity is not device-dependent.

— *Bruce Mau*

Think Like a Pro

The thinking processes we all use every day are many and varied. Composing a letter takes a different kind of thinking than designing a doghouse or creating a menu for dinner or making the perfect football play on the fly. Each of these everyday acts of thinking, no matter how conscious or subconscious, draws on the imagination and is manifested in time and space.

Sometimes thinking processes get formalized and taught to achieve specific results. The scientific method is one of these — making an educated guess about an answer to a question, called a hypothesis, then moving through a controlled experiment to see if your hypothesis is correct, then doing it again and again to determine if the results are repeatable.

Another is algebra. While we don't really call it a thinking process, it is a method for solving a problem. You could extend this analogy to many everyday activities: cooking, riding a bike, making a budget, etc. Many things you do each day might be so practiced that they seem to happen on "automatic pilot." In fact, a series of thinking steps is occurring in your brain to guide your actions.

When we learn to do something new, moving through the step-by-step process is a conscious activity. Remember learning how to drive? Putting all the right thinking pieces in the right order is important: the seat belt fastened, mirrors adjusted, ignition on, parking brake off, right gear, looking out, measuring space with your eyes, then just the right amount of pressure on the pedal with your foot, and so on. It took lots of practice to gain expertise over time. Now much of the thinking process for driving has probably gone "underground," but it still happens.

The creative process of thinking is the same. It's not only a thinking process, but a method of work. And we can learn it just by following the steps. It isn't used often in school because in school, the desired results are already known — and more easily measured. But here we're going to break it down into its basic steps: **collecting, playing, creating, and reflecting.**

A note about "ideas"...
When we use the word "idea" we mean impulse or notion, not necessarily a full-blown plan.

When we can plug into our unique brand of creative thinking, it's like finding our "sweet spot." It is a superhighway for ideas, straight from the imagination. It's where we do our most fluent and flexible thinking. When we have to think from a place that's not our own, it can be difficult. You may have been asked to learn a dance when you were born with "two left feet," or to follow a verbal map when what you really needed was a picture, or maybe your drawing was *not* put up on the bulletin board in second grade and you assumed you were deficient. It's happened to all of us in different ways. And it happens to children every day who may be part of the majority who don't naturally think linearly and abstractly, and then get the impression they are "dumb."

We need all these ways of thinking to be honored and practiced if we want truly creative thinking. It's up to parents to fill this bill for their kids. Start by using the creative process of thinking consciously, like you do when you use the scientific method as you approach a science experiment. Here it is:

The Creative Process

1. Collecting or gathering ideas – this can mean anything from making a word list to collecting different shapes of seashells, or keeping a file of images and quotes that appeal to you.

2. Playing – combining and recombining bits from your collection, adding other media and "what ifs"...letting your imagination have full reign.

3. Creating – this is where you begin to select, edit, polish, taking your ideas and making some kind of form. This could be as simple as a sandwich, or as big and complex as a symphony.

4. Reflecting – when you are really creating, one answer leads to another idea, or to another question. What happened? Did it work? What next? Now you're off down a fertile and interesting path.

Creating With Kids

Ask for creative work from your children. Put out some "scratch" materials and present a problem to solve that is appropriate for the developmental stage of the child. It might be place cards for dinner, a "surprise" game for a toddler, an organizer for the back of the seat of the car, or a new cover for the phone book. It might not be something "useful." How about a sound machine, the most interesting digital photo that shows "speed", or a paper doll dress from the best color of pink in six magazines?

Share the steps of the creative thinking process with children who are old enough to get it. It can be really helpful for a child to know that "collecting ideas" is separate from "creating/making" and deserves time and attention all its own. Lead the younger ones. Be patient with the process. Allow plenty of time for the collecting and playing part.

Then let creating happen. The result won't be what you would have done, no doubt. It may not be exactly what would solve the problem best. But consciously exercising the process is worth the time and effort. It's like reading: it takes time and practice. And adults help children along by presenting an interesting challenge at the right time.

Reflect on the process with your child. Let your imaginations wander down the path of *what ifs* — other materials, sizes, timing? What questions or new ideas come to mind? Does this experience generate a "let's try this next"?

Enjoy knowing that all the experiments and original ideas will be tucked away in the back pocket of a young imagination, to be sorted and resorted, maybe taken apart and remembered in some new, likely hidden, way by a growing and evolving mind at work.

The following pages give you some specific ideas to work with:

A Step-By-Step Guide for Parents Through the Creative Process:

Making a Study

(appropriate for ages 4 and older)

To put this process in concrete terms, here is an exercise using different materials and different starting ideas to take you and your child through the process together. One of the truths about this process is that the more the original idea is interesting and intriguing to the child, the more it is something he or she can sink teeth into, and the better the process works. The next few pages illustrate a simple study with specific content and a specific format direction. The payoff for your child will most likely come when you set up a study that honors a subject your child is passionate about – maybe even obsessed about.

Put yourself – the grownup – in the supporting cast, follow your child and let his or her ideas and natural inclinations lead the process. Remember that these are just jumping off places for an investigative study. As you and your child – or your child alone – work through some of these exercises, you may decide to change the rules in midstream, following one idea that pops up into a totally unexpected form of its own. The magic of an idea-to-form process is, indeed, its very nonlinear and unpredictable nature. By learning to pay close attention along the way, throughout the process, children learn to find the "right" form, the best and most fitting form for ideas. As parents mentoring this process, we can best support it by providing the tools and materials that are called for, acting as a supportive audience providing feedback by listening and paying attention, and by getting out of the way and letting the child have a go at it.

MAKING A "FAVORITES" STUDY

STEP 1: COLLECTING IDEAS

Start a conversation about favorites and look for them in everyday spaces. Share yours and find out your child's. Starting points: favorite clothes, favorite shoes, favorite window view, favorite tree, favorite place to hide, favorite words, favorite dance, and then, favorite colors, textures, shapes, spaces...using the sensory alphabet as a jumping off point.

Your child draws, using markers or colored pencils or watercolors, simple sketches and painting impressions of these favorites. You label with appropriate narrative: "My favorite blue hat," "A favorite line," "My favorite space for naps." Cut or tear pictures from magazines or take digital photos and print them. The goal: to compile a good collection of all kinds and categories of favorites. Or you can concentrate on just one category, such as favorite colors.

STEP 2: PLAYING WITH AN IDEA —
a.k.a. BRAINSTORMING

Ask your child to pick his or her most interesting or most intriguing idea about favorites from this bigger collection—it could be one idea with several categories, such as favorite colors, or a single favorite thing. Try the following playful approaches to generate even more images and information. With younger children you can have a "what if" conversation to play with the ideas and then encourage your child to draw, write or otherwise record the ideas and images that come to mind. With older kids, you might even make up a "study" notebook of envelopes and blank pages for him or her to use to chart the process.

MAKE IT BIGGER
What if everything in the world was your favorite color? What if your favorite blue hat was big enough for you to live inside? What if your favorite space was big enough for a hundred of you?

MAKE IT SMALLER
What if only you had a tiny piece of paper with a tiny splash of your favorite color – and no one else had ever seen this color? What if your favorite blue hat could be worn by an ant? What if your favorite space was big enough for you, but only if you were the size of a peanut?

LOOK AT THE OPPOSITE
What is the opposite color of your favorite color? Why do you think so? What would happen if everything in the world were painted this color? Could your favorite blue hat be

turned into blue shoes? What if everyone wore blue shoes? What are the qualities that describe your favorite space – what are the opposite qualities and what kind of space would they make? How would you feel in this opposite kind of space?

CHANGE YOUR VIEWPOINT
Tell the life story of your favorite color: I am green... I live in a ....I eat.... Draw pictures of your favorite blue hat from every perspective, above, below, close to, from far away, through a microscope. Draw a map of your favorite space as though it were a city, a playground, a country all its own.

MAKE A MATCH
Match your favorite color to these categories: food, sounds, times of day. Imagine adding the following to your favorite blue hat: feathers, strings, giraffe head, water, fruit. What if your favorite space was also filled with your favorite textures? Imagine your favorite space matched to these inhabitants: an alien, a dinosaur, a ferocious lion, a tiny pet.

ADD OTHER ELEMENTS
Mentally or with materials explore your idea favorites consciously using the language of invention. What happens when you add your favorite color to different textures? What happens to your favorite space in different kinds of light? What if that favorite blue hat was transformed into 100 different shapes?

STEP 3: CREATING —
a.k.a. SYNTHESIS TO FORM

By this time more than one of these ideas will have started to sprout wings. An attentive parent can help guide the process by providing feedback and help with selection and matching to age- and skill-appropriate materials and media. Younger children can simply select and organize sketches and transcribed stories into a notebook or scrapbook. Older children may want to tackle a simple handmade book. There are many other decisions to make along the way that will affect the final look and style, including the kind of illustration materials (colored pencils, markers, oil pastel drawings watercolors, cutout or torn paper collage, digital photos or snapshots, etc). Experiment with a variety of media.

Some approaches that may help include:
- Arranging ideas into different kinds of categories
- Making a connected story with a selection of ideas
- Putting sketches and words into a template of
    grids or columns.
- Trying a Japanese folding book format
- Designing a page or two to check how the ideas
    look in different formats of size and shape.
- Making a "thumbnail" of tiny pictures of each
    page so that you see how the whole book
    will flow before you fill out each page.

STEP 3.5: POLISHING YOUR CREATION

Sometimes children will want to stop with STEP 3. Other times, a child will want to go further. For a presentation to an audience, almost any innovative effort can benefit from a bit of polish. Including this as a conscious part of the invention of a form gives children experience in mastery. Sometimes, a bit of parent-furnished polish gives children's work the presence it needs to help the child see his or her own idea's excellence. Sometimes, an adult's helpful technical skills or better-developed motor skills are needed to make a form shine. Straight lines are sometimes called for.

With word forms, you may want to help your child make sure the spelling and grammar are correct to keep the communication clear. With illustrations, kids can "clean up" their work by gluing final illustrations onto clean bordered sheets, erasing pencil guidelines, etc. Polishing gets more sophisticated with age, but we think that kids' work deserves to be treated with respect. Sometimes, a project that has taken more effort and time — such as the one described in this study process — will deserve more than a temporary home on the refrigerator door.

STEP 4: REFLECTING

This part of the process involves looking back over all the ideas that were collected, but not used this time: the experiments with materials that provided ideas about others to try, themes and favorites to expand on with new idea additions or new materials. Notice choices your child made (or rejected), ideas that sparked smiles. Mull. Take notes. Make plans for jumping off points for next time. This part of the process is for you to do alone and also to share with your child. Building in habits of reflection helps young inventors step back into a bigger, more analytical picture that can help build creative momentum.

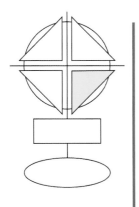

Individuality:
Turbo-Charging
the Process

*The most important thing
is to know what you're good at.*

— Peter Drucker

One of a Kind

We come into this world as unique individuals. Every parent with more than one child will absolutely attest to this fact. The things we notice first as parents are these telling traits: a baby who is a mover, full of physical energy, can't be still; a calm baby who needs to sit back and watch everything before joining in; a social baby who loves to engage in interactions with people. These characteristics seem to be indelible as we grow up. How many times have we heard parents recounting tales of their children who were "just like this" from babyhood?

In the last 20 years, notions of inborn individual differences have been supported by the research of pediatricians, developmental psychologists and cognitive scientists. The groundbreaking work of Drs. Jerome Bruner, T. Berry Brazelton, Howard Gardner and Mel Levine, among many others, all speak to these issues from the perspectives of their various fields. In our research with children over the years at Learning About Learning, we used a child's creative work along with behavioral patterns, viewed through a sensory lens, to discern these differences.

These unique configurations of individual differences permeate the many layers that add up to our unique identities and relate to far more than personality. They show how we naturally perceive the world, how we process information, how we create meaning. Finally, they show what we are naturally good at doing. These particular constellations of qualities make up our individual strengths. We all have them. When our strengths happen to coincide with what our culture says is "cool" or important, we call it talent!

Think of the singers, the gymnasts, the painters.

When we (adults AND children) are working from our strengths, we are doing our most satisfying (and creative) work. It is like having our own personal compass. We are going with the flow. Working from strength, we find it easy to generate ideas, to sail along on an internal fountain of energy and do good work. It is what we strive for as we look for our direction in the world.

When we are NOT working from strength, we often experience low self esteem, stress, and burnout. But discovering our strengths is an endeavor that is most often left until adulthood. And even then, figuring out how we get to that creative career where we shine, that "sweet spot," is often left to chance. And then it can be a lonely trial-and-error process.

It's enormously helpful to start finding our strengths earlier in life. And of course, here parents are key. Looking for a child's natural strengths is far easier when we disengage our old ways of thinking from the usual institutional templates. Sharpening our sensory perception is what is needed. (Remember ESP? EXTRA sensory perception? Well, this is "SP" — Sensory Perception!)

Here, we want to show you some visual evidence in children — of how individual differences look and how the patterns show themselves in a child's creative work. The photographs on the following pages were taken during a course for 5-year-olds called "New World Kids," at the Aldrich Contemporary Museum in Ridgefield, Connecticut in the summer of 2007.

Seeing Imaginations at Work

There were a dozen "New World Kids" participating and, of course, there are a dozen, unique stories and profiles. The two-week course consisted of:

- learning the Sensory Alphabet
- building observation skills
- practicing the creative process
- having a variety of media experiences
- hearing from adults about their own thinking and working processes

Along the way, we were noticing the children's individual differences and documenting their work. After a few days, patterns began to emerge. We will use the Sensory Alphabet here as a lens to demonstrate those patterns. We've chosen three children for this chapter whose imaginations can be readily contrasted in print. Meet these three children:

Henry is very spatially oriented, in a 3-D sense. His work demonstrates this understanding. He sees and makes strong shapes. Henry is interested in balance and symmetry and repeatedly chooses to work with few shapes and colors.

Grace loves texture. Her favorite ways of working always include layers and multiple media whenever possible. The tactile qualities of the materials are important, and for Gracie, more is always better.

Pedro is very visual, and his work is very linear. He loves filling 2-D graphic space with line drawings of the movies that are playing in his mind. He is a natural story teller — another linear format. (At 5, he needs a secretary to record the stories that complete his work.)

1st Clue:

On SPACE day, the children chose one of the small figures to represent themselves and created a shape and size of space that felt comfortable. The media were clay and straws.

Note: These next pages are examples of "open-ended activities" — ones that call forth personal and creative responses from the child. There are no right answers, no copying. These were their different interpretations:

Henry

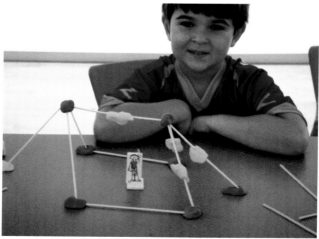

Henry quickly and intuitively created a space made with triangles. It was simple and stable and showcased his natural understanding of working with 3-D elements.

Grace

Grace created a cube, a shape that probably came more from an idea of a space, a mental construct, that was then translated (with a bit of help) into a space for her tiny pretend "self."

Pedro

Pedro "did not compute." His extremely 2-D orientation made it difficult for him to imagine a 3-D space. And he was not being silly or acting up. This is a vital clue to the shape of Pedro's imagination.

2nd clue:

On COLOR day, a designer visited the class, brought colored yarns and talked about the process of designing clothes. He also brought an activity — designing a shirt. The children worked on a template with markers. Here are their designs, and what became apparent about their individual styles:

Henry

Henry used the linear media (markers) to create shapes and used only two colors — on purpose.

Grace

Grace created a texture design here. Clearly, she could stay inside the lines if she chose (check the pink collar), but she was expressing tactile information.

Pedro

Pedro chose lines, his favorite element, carefully filling the space with no overlapping. He also included many colors.

3rd Clue:

On TEXTURE day, one of the activities was making collages, with many materials offered. These three children had strikingly different responses:

Henry

Henry responded with a few hard-edged shapes. The balanced and symmetrical placement was important, and his choice of materials seemed more related to the shape of the objects than their tactile qualities.

Grace

Grace really enjoyed making a collage. She chose elements that had a strong tactile quality and then layered them. Her work was full of texture.

Pedro

Pedro's idea of a collage was more like a classification system. He placed his chosen elements in rows (lines) and nothing overlapped.

4th Clue:

Along the way, the New World Kids worked on "me papers" when we had time — life-sized tracings of each kid that they filled in with all kinds of personal favorites, using writing or drawing. On the last day, we finished them and added paint to the available media choices. This is how they turned out:

Henry

Henry colored in his clothes as big shapes
(not easy when you're working with markers)
and stayed carefully inside the lines for definition.
You can see he is a Red Sox fan from the
little red shapes on his shirt.

80

Grace

Gracie worked all over the paper and was delighted to figure out that she could slide things under the paper, making rubbings to create a textural effect. She cut out colored shapes and pasted them on too.

Pedro

Pedro chose one area of the figure to fill with a drawing that made a story. He was happy to use markers only and liked the bright, graphic colors. (The drawing in the upper left corner shows his drafting skill.)

5th Clue:

On the last day, the children were allowed to select their favorite media and create freely. The results added to the individual profiles of their unique styles of thinking and working. Their differences continued to show:

Henry

Henry created a 3-D sculpture, a strong and simple shape using three colors.

Grace

Grace's final project was a collage with many materials and layers. Here she is, at work on it with her tape in hand.

Pedro

Since Pedro was barely five and couldn't write yet, he needed an assistant for his final project — an elaborate story, illustrated with his line drawings.

Henry

Henry's 3-D skills and interest in balance might foreshadow a rewarding career in architecture, engineering or construction. A "mind-feeding" project could be to design and build a doghouse or a treehouse with an architectural student.

Grace

Grace's love of texture needs "hands on" media. Many fields accent the tactile sensibility that Gracie has in abundance — cooking, weaving, surgery, or maybe clothing or garden design.

.

Pedro

Pedro's very strong visual and linear imagination, paired with his drawing skill, would make him a natural animation artist or possibly a video game designer. That same linear quality, along with his love of storytelling, might transfer into to words when he goes to school and he might like to become a writer or journalist.

Adding It Up

The individual style of each child's pattern of thinking and creating is consistent and distinct, and it is something that will continue throughout their lifetimes. These patterns show us where their natural imaginations are most fluent and most satisfying. They also give beginning indications of what media, fields of study and even careers the children might enjoy.

But notably, the institution of education today would usually reward only Pedro's linear sensibility. Henry's skills at shape and space or Grace's strong textural sense are not on the radar screen of what is important at school. And the danger is that these championship children can easily be defined by school and grades — and feel that they are lacking when they are not. Identities can be at stake for young children.

Again, this is where parents come in, locating their children's natural strengths, mirroring them back to their children and valuing them. Parents can teach creative thinking and make home a place where each individual's creativity is practiced, valued and supported.

For now, each of these children would benefit from playing with materials that support their individual constellation of strengths. As they get a bit older and can become aware of and centered in their strengths, they can begin to take more responsibility for their own learning — knowing which subjects may be more difficult and which will be "a breeze." For example, a "linear, 2-D" kid may do well with the linear qualities of algebra, but find visualizing the 3-D shapes of solid geometry more difficult. The sensory vocabulary is a central tool for analyzing the qualities of fields of study and matching them with children's strengths.

In the context of every day, as a child grows older and develops an increased capacity for reflection, the "subject" of individual strengths can be a shared and ongoing investigation between parents and children. It can be a source of inspiration — for example, on a family vacation: Who enjoys research? Who's best at logistics? Who likes navigating? Who's best at assembling the picnic basket?

Parents can find their children like-minded mentors that inspire them with new experiences and fields of study that parents wouldn't have thought of when their own native styles don't match. Conversely, when a child is confident and centered in his or her strengths, it can be a valuable to "crew" for an expert in a field that really doesn't match— to observe, try on and try out a really different kind of mindset and experience a "stretch."

Big projects, like putting on a play or creating an exhibition, present the need to call on more than one viewpoint. It's a good opportunity for kids to analyze how to best use each other's strengths. (Who can be the lighting director? Who does the business and takes the tickets? Who designs the costumes? Who writes the story? Who does the advertising?)

In short, we believe it's important for parents to start to identify their children's strengths early. This careful consideration is a very special ingredient that parents can add to their child's development, amplifying a child's creativity with thoughtfully selected materials, custom-designed activities and like-minded resources.

Parents know and love their children best. They have their children's long-term interests at heart. Parents can sense strengths in their child that may not match the criteria someone else, like a teacher or coach, is using. The following pages provide a palette of questions, grouped in different categories, for parents to ask themselves about their child — ways of contrasting and comparing qualities to bring them into a higher focus.

Assessing Your Child's Strengths

One-on-one.
One-of-a-kind.

Each of our children is absolutely unrepeatable. If you have more than one, you already know this. If you spend 15 minutes watching at the playground, you'll know it. If you look at a stack of drawings from a group of 6-year-olds, you'll see the differences, given a few tools for looking.

How do you look at your child with new eyes, outside of the daily get-dones and to-dos? It helps to have a certain distance, an anthropologist's viewpoint. Step beyond judgment (this is good; this is bad) into a position of value-free observation. It often helps to use comparative information. Sometimes it's easiest to see your child's unique combo plate when it's sitting on the table next to another kid's menu choices. Here's a checklist to help you observe, collect and compare.

Observing Actions

Start with observation. Use a camera to catch typical actions and behaviors, or just reflect and write.

How does my child sound? What's his voice like? Do you

hear the clumping or tiptoeing or trotting of her feet through space? Is this a child with soft or strong sound qualities? Is he talking fast or mulling things over before he speaks? Is she a story always in the telling, or a dramatic announcer of all things important?

How does my child move? Is she a whirlwind at the center of any activity or a slow observer who has to watch before jumping in? Does he have wings on his feet and a kinesthetic grasp of each and every movement through space? Or not? Do you note a facility with hand-eye coordination, or do you have a kid whose favorite exercise is mental gymnastics? Does she fidget and wiggle her way through the day, daintily twirl at every opportunity, or cut through space with conviction, ignoring obstacles and rules at every turn?

What is the rhythm of my child? If I clapped a rhythmic score, would it be regular and evenly paced? Or erratic and unpredictable? Would she be a march or a tango? A jive or a three-ring circus? Is he fast, slow, somewhere in between? Surprising or forthright?

How does my child use her face and eyes? Is this one an open book or a mysterious stranger who seldom lets his emotions show? Is drama the operative word or is methodical her method? What happens when my child meets a stranger? Is he out in the game or on the sideline keeping score?

How does my child present a public face? Is it different from the private life I see as a parent? How do others respond to my child?

What kind of roles and functions does my child take on? Alpha dog? Follower? Listener? Starring role? Backstage director? Conformist? Devil's advocate?

What makes him laugh? What makes her funny? Where's his funny bone? What brings her joy? What is sure to bring a smile to his face?

What questions does he ask over and over and over again? Is she a "What?" or a "Why?" a "How do I?" or a "What if I?" What makes his viewpoint different from anyone else's? One-of-a-kind?

Preferences

Another way to collect information about your child is to note preferences – the things she collects, chooses, concentrates her efforts on. Here's a second checklist of observations and inventories to make.

What catches his eye? Movement? Color? Light and shadow? Strong patterns? Interesting shapes? Or is it all about touch? Or movement? Or telling the story?

What holds her attention? What things does she do for longer than other children? Music? Building and construction toys? Puzzles or books? Art-making or role-playing?

What does he surround himself with? The choices for toys, for his room, for activities? Is it other people? Animals? Things to build with? Stuff that moves?

What qualities do her favorite games and toys have? Are they all big or small movement activities? Do they have procedures or linear rules? Do you see strong sensuous qualities, tactile elements or sound and motion? How about emotional or analytic components?

What does he collect? What gets picked up on the street

or on the playground? Rocks and shells? Magazines, bugs, or little glittery bits of foil and glass? If she could make a collection of anything, would it be hats or robots, ribbons or sports equipment? Does he find and save photos, maps or cartoons? Character dolls or jokes?

What kinds of things — especially in a new place or space — is my child most likely to comment about? The people or the colors? The sound or the story? The size or the materials? The construction and engineering or the aesthetics and theatrical sense? What does she pick up? Save? Store? Ask about or comment on?

Materials

What are the qualities of the materials that my child likes best? Track these favorites through the sensory alphabet!

COLOR: Are these materials colorful or monochromatic? What kinds of colors? Bright or subtle? Dark or light? Contrasting or soothing? One child may *have* to have that new box of crayons, while another just needs a big black permanent marker.

TEXTURE: How do the materials your child likes feel to the touch? Are they smooth or nubby, plastic or hard, malleable or rigid, natural or manmade? Is that collection of stuffed animals a textural necessity or a cast of characters for bed-top drama?

SHAPE: Do these materials — toys, games, art media, favorite objects — have definite shapes? Or are they ambiguous or amorphous? Are they simple in contour or intricate? Do they have structural parts or components? Is a morning in a sand pile or a day in the sand at the beach the ultimate entertainment?

MOVEMENT: Do her favorite materials move or have movement implicit in them? Is there a rhythm to them or to their use? Is the movement smooth, fast or floating? Humorous, serious or unstable? Does your child simply have to move no matter what or where?

SOUND: Do these favorites make sounds, either by design or by your child's use? What kind of sound quality — musical or percussive, wind or string, whistling or thudding? Is there a definite rhythm to the sound produced? Does your child make sounds with things that no one else would ever think to turn into an instrument?

RHYTHM: Are they stacked or patterned? Put in order or grouped? Repeated or reorganized over and over? Put away in categories or lumped together any old way? Is there a rhythm to her play, a beginning, middle and end? Do word play or rhymes have a particular charm?

LINE: Do these favorite materials have a linear quality? Are they curved or angular? Strongly directional, repetitive or meandering? Is there always a storyline going on, a movie in the mind?

LIGHT: Is this material one that has qualities of light, dark, opacity, transparency? Does he play with light and shadow? Like to create an environmental "mood"?

SPACE: What spatial qualities do the materials have? Are these favorite materials two-dimensional or three-dimensional (i.e., given a choice does your child choose clay or paper and pen?) What's the scale she likes to work with — a desktop or a playing field, tiny miniatures or large brushes and a six-foot-tall roll of paper?

Other Aspects

What spaces and places does he prefer for free play? Is she always on the porch or in her bedroom? Alone in the backyard or in the kitchen with everyone else? Does she need a run in the park to stay healthy and sane? Is time alone essential? Or is time spent with a group mandatory and energizing?

When we interact, is it playful or serious? Directive? Organized? Improvisational?

When we work together on a task, does she stay on track or need to come and go? Does he need a process or a product? Does she have to know why, or why not? Where's the payoff?

When we play, does she want to be the boss of you? Or watch and follow? Is he open to coaching or resistant to change? Does she worry about getting it "right"? Is he making up new rules as we go along? Or sticking to a strategy?

Take some time to "add up" the qualities you see. Begin to see your child as a mind at work. What kinds of materials would really feed this mind? What people do you know who might make wonderful mentors? What projects could really expand this special brand of creativity?

Part 2:

Ideas
in Motion

Creating Everyday

A single day is enough to make us a little larger.

— *Paul Klee*

Putting It All Together

You've seen the material at hand — your child's unrepeatable mind. Given that your child's individuality is the content, what's the context? We share the same 24 hours each day, whatever happens happens within that frame. Time is the space we fill with to-dos and tah-dahs, tasks and tidbits, routines and rituals. Ideally, these get us through each day with grace. We accomplish what has to be done — clothes, meals, cleaning, comfort, homework, carpools, calendars, the daily juggle of work, play and rest — and also take time to nurture that unrepeatable individuality.

Made up of day-to-day actions, some in-place reactions, and the occasional special celebration, time spent with our children is truly unrepeatable. Mindfulness and intent, as well as improvisation, carry a lot of weight for parents, since each day we face someone a little bit older, a little bit wiser, a little bit further along his or her path to independence. But along the way, we must find ways to support what is unique and special about our child's mind and creative process.

In the next few pages, you'll find some formulas for shaping the everyday, exercising parental creativity along the way. We're not trying for an all-encompassing compendium — just providing a few starters to get the gears going.

Shaping the Routine

Sure, you want life to be full of surprises, but does bedtime have to be reinvented nightly? Do you really have the energy for every buckle-up to be a battle? Daily routines and rituals promote peace and let you and your child put energy where it's really needed. Not every routine works for every child. Understanding your child's individuality can help shape routines and rituals that keep the wheels turning more easily.

Answer these questions in order to build routines that work for you and your child:

Are transitions always an issue? What could be designed as "warning bells" or "countdowns" if your child has problems making shifts from one activity to another? Does a movement break help? Or does your child need a chance to stop, look and listen?

Kids love secret signals and signs. What kind of signal can be designed ahead of time – a gesture, a word, a phrase – to stand in for one of those parental warnings? Make this secret language an invention project for the family. Use a signal that your child will notice based on his communication strengths.

How could you honor your child's strong suits in daily tasks such as cleaning up toys, making the bed, taking part in meal preparations, getting homework done? A child with a strong sense of rhythm might enjoy timed tasks or racing the clock; a child who responds to space probably needs well-defined places to put things and a special area for homework tasks. A child who loves color and shape could take on the dinner table as an art project (just make sure the take-down is part of the deal).

What kinds of chores really make sense for your child's mind? Don't let what you think is age- or gender-appropriate outweigh a child's real abilities and interests. If your child loves small-motor work and is competent with tools, add more sophisticated cooking tasks. If he loves big movement, turn him loose on raking the yard or cleaning windows with a long-handled squeegee. If she's detail oriented, make her the official keeper-of-the-calendar. Find real work for children to do, and appreciate their contributions.

What kinds of bedtime rituals fit your life and your child? How could this be a special time for communication in a way that honors individuality? Bedtime could mean storytelling together, poems read, music for the mood, slow stretches.

Tackle other day-to-day tasks by inventorying the materials at hand, your familial goals, whether the task needs to go on auto-pilot or whether the particular task has room inside of it for your child to exercise his or her creative imagination. Take time to shape the day-to-day routines that make up your everyday. "Everyday" really is the material you have to work with.

Home, a Place for Ideas

Here are some ideas to make your home a place that shelters AND extends your child's mind at work.

Spaces for Collections

Where can your child save, share and catalog his "sensory alphabet" collections? Try little pin boards and wall-sized bulletin boards, collection cubbies, shelves, a pedestal or shadowbox for changing displays, and other special areas. Honor each person's collections in revolving "exhibits" in your home.

Think digitally. Schedule photo-sharing night for digital collection reviews, or buy an inexpensive digital photo frame to share a child's collection of lines, shapes or colors. Set up an area on the family computer for each person's photo collection. Take time to make periodic photo books either with your own print-outs or using one of the online photo book programs.

Design your child's room as space for a mind at work. Plan and build it together. Does he need room to move and levels to move through? Does she need lots of table space and a wall-mounted roll of 36-inch-wide paper for drawing? Does she need a hard surface for building toys and construction sets? Does he need lots of pegs and hangers for a collection of hats and costumes for dramatic play? What kind of books and media need to be at hand? What kind of raw materials and tools? Look through school furnishing and school supply catalogs for ideas and resources beyond the department store children's furnishings.

Investigate outdoor options. Whether you have a large yard and garden, a city apartment pocket space or just a balcony, investigate the options to fit your child's imagination and opportunity for invention. What if you invented wind chimes, sun-catchers, a tree house, sandbox or table? Obstacle course or game field? Secret hiding spot, outdoor stage, camping tent and campfire pit?

Everyday Spaces for Media and Play

As you design your home, choose furnishing for children's rooms, and design spaces for your child's play in the home, pay more attention to what's really going on – or needs to go on – than to what a decorator might suggest. Themed bedrooms and playrooms may be popular, but make sure that the theme has something to do with your child's imagination. Most kids need a space for messy play – outdoors or in. Many children need ways to move differently within their living spaces. Some kids need specialized spaces for collections, for tools, for building toys or costumes.

Excursions and Outings

Here's just one example. Use it as a template to design your own.

TEN WAYS TO GO TO THE ZOO
(Activities for Parents and Children)

1. Take a small sketch book with pen and draw the most interesting shapes and lines you see. Translate one or more into large simple pillows for your child's room, using fabric bonding material or simple appliqué.

2. During your visit take turns leading each other on a "blindfolded" walk so that you each concentrate on the information you discover with your ears and through your feet.

3. Imitate big and little movements you see animals make, walking like one animal as you move to the next animal enclosure.

---

4. Go at feeding time and discover the mealtime rhythm of the zoo.

5. Spend extra time at a few animal areas, each family member choosing at least one animal to "turn into" a human character. Imagine what clothes it would wear, how the character would walk, talk and interact. On the way home, or later, turn your cast of characters into a skit or story.

6. Using a simple camera, collect animal patterns or colors or textures.

7. Collect sounds on a small tape recorder. Record your imitation of the sounds you hear. Listen later and write a vocal song or, if you can, input your collection into a computer to manipulate as material for a musical composition.

8. Take watercolors and paper and make paintings of animals in their environments.

9. Have each family member chooses one animal before the zoo visit to research on the internet or in books, becoming the expert guide for that species and sharing the information when you see the animal.

10. Imagine the zoo of the future or the ideal zoo of today. Discuss design ideas with each other.

Celebrations

Birthdays, holidays, important accomplishments – these are the times that you want to be special. In the sea of days, these are the big fish – the times we hope our children will remember forever. Sometimes this impulse leads us to the craziness of extreme consumerism and one-upmanship. How much better they would be, if we could make them the standout moments designed for our child's imagination? The idea is to create the kind of time that is richly sensory and vivid.

Think about these questions, first without regard for budget, practicality or reality, purely brainstorming with your child's mind at the center.

What place would be the most exciting place for this child? Where in the world (or the galaxy) would she want to visit?

What tools or materials would be perfect for your child? If he were an adult, what might those tools and materials be? Who would you like this child to have time with? Who would she like to talk with, dance with, paint with, read with, explore with?

What size group is best for this child?

What kind of interactions does he like best – one-on-one, being the leader, watching and observing – and how could this impulse be part of an event?

Now, take your brainstorm answers and turn the impulse into a party, an outing or excursion, an event or experience that includes the essential elements you've described. For example, maybe you can't swing a trip to an African jungle for your child, but you could take a small group to a nearby safari park with cameras for collecting animal ideas. Perhaps a telescope is too sophisticated and too expensive a gift for your 7-year-old (not to mention impractical for any city dweller), but inexpensive binoculars for a moon-watching party at the park along with a trip to a kid-friendly planetary IMAX show or planetarium might just fit the bill.

What Do You Need To Do With Your Child?

Talk? Listen? Imagine? Collect rocks, leaves, stamps or sounds? Experiment? Work? Play? Exercise? Build? Cook? Sew? Draw? Knit? Act? Paste? Sing? Design? Dance? Write? Read? Pretend? Practice? Remember? Laugh? Photograph? Tell stories? Climb? Run? Garden? Paint? Play drums? You don't need to be an expert. You don't need to know much more than your child does (and you may know even less when you hit on one of her strong suits). Do what you think she will love using the clues you collect from your own observations and intuitions.

Part 3:

Learn Your Alphabet

The Sensory Alphabet: Its Elements

All credibility, all good conscience,
all evidence of truth come only from the senses.

— Friedrich Nietzsche

Color •
Line •
Shape •
Sound •
Texture •
Light •
Movement •
Space •
Rhythm •

The following pages are
getting-to-know-you mini-chapters
for each element in the Sensory Alphabet.
This is an opportunity for looking,
comparing, contrasting and
collecting impressions —
observing where each element
appears in your own life; considering
which are your favorites and how you use them
every day. We've included quotes from writers
and others regarding each element. Activities
at the end of each mini-chapter will give you some
references for experimenting, and some
ways to explore this perceptual
language with your child.

Color

Color Words: red, blue, yellow, green, orange, purple, variegated, neutral, beige, complementary, tint, analogous, technicolor, intensity, rainbow, vivid, camouflage, deep, pastel, achromatic, pale, ochre, bright, washed-out, glaze, flat, semi-flat, indigo, gloss, violet, scarlet, rosy, chartreuse, mauve, rust, inky, snow, madder, white, dichromatic, earthy, fluorescent, metallic, gray.

everyday

nature

architecture

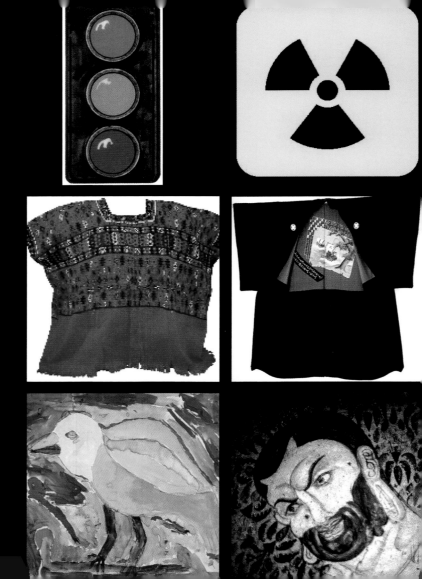

These can be done freq
Provide priming experi
Provide the best materi
Assign idea to give form
Provide a process, proc
Have students share the
Have students reflect or

Color

COLOR investigations
to do on your own:

1. What colors do you wear? What colors do you avoid wearing? For one day wear an unexpected color. (Borrow an outfit if nothing in your closet is outside your usual palette.)

2. Make a collection of small crystals to hang in a sunny window. Enjoy the tiny rainbows that flash and glimmer in your room.

3. Paint or draw with pastels to a favorite piece of classical music. Don't worry about making it "work," just play with the colors that come to mind.

4. One form of synesthesia is that people perceive words or numbers or sounds as colors. Imagine that you have this neurologic gift and envision what colors you perceive as people speak to you.

5. Take a watercolor class or try to follow the instructions in one of the many watercolor technique books on the market. You only need to purchase a primary set of watercolors to develop a broad palette. One secret to successful watercolor painting is purchasing the best paper you can afford.

6. Investigate the natural history of a favorite color. How has technology made that hue available as a dye or paint? What is its emotional connotation in different cultures? How is it used symbolically in literature, poetry and musical lyrics?

COLOR investigations to do with your child:

1. Dye eggs, even if it's not Easter.

2. Finger paint (with various kinds of paints, with different colored puddings, with shaving cream tinted with food color, with mud and earth).

3. Tint juice and other beverages with food colorings. How cool is it to drink blue milk?

4. Tie dye a shirt (use the newer dyes and tiedye paints found in the craft store for no-bleed success).

5. Paint each other's faces using makeup crayons or face paint.

6. Make "lookers" – frames or even cardboard tubes with different colored "lenses" to look through. Give different ones to your child to use during waits and trips and routine journeys. Give new meaning to rose-colored glasses.

7. Dismantle an inexpensive kaleidoscope and then invent a new one with better parts.

8. Paint one wall of your child's room with his or her absolutely favorite color and let your child help. If you can't paint, hang a stretched panel of fabric –as though it were a large painting.

9. Help your child start a color collection, filling a scrapbook with examples of a favorite color: photos, magazine collage, packaging, paper scraps, etc.

10. Collect fall leaves and preserve their colors by dipping them in melted paraffin, for young children, copy them on a color copier.

11. Color code your child's toys and other possessions matching them to a color-coded room map or to color-coded storage bins and shelves. Turn clean-up into a color match game.

Talking About Color:

The Mediterranean has the color of mackerel, changeable I mean. You don't always know if it is green or violet, you can't even say it's blue, because the next moment the changing reflection has taken on a tint of rose or gray.

— Vincent van Gogh

White...is not a mere absence of colour; it is a shining and affirmative thing, as fierce as red, as definite as black... God paints in many colours; but He never paints so gorgeously, I had almost said so gaudily, as when He paints in white.

— *G. K. Chesterton*

Color is the place where our brain and the universe meet.

— Paul Klee

I found I could say things with color and shapes that I couldn't say any other way — things I had no words for.

— *Georgia O'Keeffe*

The sound of colors is so definite that it would be hard to find anyone who would express bright yellow with bass notes or dark lake with treble...

— Wassily Kandinsky

If one says "Red" (the name of color) and there are fifty people listening, it can be expected that there will be fifty reds in their minds. And one can be sure that all these reds will be very different.

— *Josef Albers*

Line

Line words:
Straight	Long
Crooked	Parallel
Skinny	Diagonal
Jagged	Vertical
Curved	Border
Spiral	Time
Looped	Circular
Twisted	Waiting
Telephone	Dotted
Date	Story
Out	Zigzag
	Checkout

everyday

nature

architecture

Line

Line

LINE investigations
to do on your own:

1. Collect a variety of pens, pencils, crayons and other mark-making tools from around the house (or buy a selection from an art store or dime store). Enjoy the sensation of filling large pieces of paper (at least 18" by 24') with lines from a tool. Which do you like best?

2. Fill sketchbook pages with an invented script or imaginary calligraphy.

3. On index cards write or sketch a list of significant events in your life. Make a series of story lines by arranging the events in different order. What would be the most interesting way to tell the story (line) of your life?

4. Buy a Japanese brush and India ink or an ink block from an art store and experiment with lines.

5. Do something backward from the way you usually do it. Start with dessert. Put your shoes on first.

6. Make a personal history time line, including events of significance in your life, your town's life, in the world situation; in art, music and culture.

7. Make a contour drawing. Set up a simple still life (or even better, ask a friend to pose for you for 10 to 15 minutes). Sketch your subject, slowly and deliberately, keeping your pencil on the paper and your eyes on the subject the entire session. Trace each contour that you see, working as if you were touching your subject with your finger or with your pencil. Do not look at your paper until you have completed the drawing.

LINE investigations
to do with your child:

1. Invent a simple secret code using lines to substitute for letters that you and your child can use to communicate.

2. Play a story line game, taking turns adding a line to an ongoing story.

3. Design a board game that uses the events in your child's life as part of its structure.

4. Together, consider the following fields of study with an eye on lines: geometry, astronomy, geology and topology,

5. Learn how to make a cat's cradle and other string games.

6. Visit a museum and look for lines in the paintings and sculptures. With paint or ink and brushes, fill pages with all kinds of lines. Draw happy line, sad lines, sleepy lines and busy lines, thick lines, thin lines, jagged lines and smooth lines.

7. Draw a simple map with your child and talk about how to go from one point to the next. Draw linear paths on your map.

8. Give your child a piece of chalk to "take a line for a walk" down a sidewalk or in an empty parking lot.

9. Make a line maze by unraveling a ball of yarn in an outdoor or indoor space. Get your child to untangle the maze and trace the line back into a ball. This is even more fun with several children and several different balls of yarn or string.

Talking About Line:

A line is a dot that went for a walk.

— Paul Klee.

What is straight? A line can be straight, or a street, but the human heart, oh, no, it's curved like a road through mountains.

— *Tennessee Williams*

When I came from horizontal vertical straight all old stuff then suddenly I go also again in curved lines. And there I submit to changes in the intensity of my hand leading a tool, you see.

— Josef Albers

The idea is to write it so that people hear it and it slides through the brain and goes straight to the heart.

—*Maya Angelou*

I realized by using the high notes of the chords as a melodic line, and by the right harmonic progression, I could play what I heard inside me. That's when I was born.

— Charlie Parker

It's a little like casting out hundreds of fishing lines into the audience. You start getting little bites, then more, then you hook a few, then more. Then you can start reeling them in and that's the loveliest feeling — the whole audience laughing with you.

—*Jim Dale*

Shape

shape words:
round • square • sinuous •
voluptuous • nebulous • angular • freeform •
triangular • vague • well-defined • inflated •
deflated • polygon • sphere • cone •
silhuoette • geometric • regular •
irregular • large • tiny • heart
shaped • narrow • solid • hollow • cube •
ball • octagonal • asymmetrical •
squashed •
ornate

everyday

nature

architecture

Shape

notations

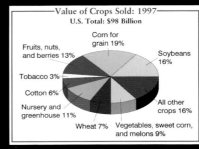

Value of Crops Sold: 1997
U.S. Total: $98 Billion

Corn for grain 19%
Soybeans 16%
Fruits, nuts, and berries 13%
Tobacco 3%
Cotton 6%
Nursery and greenhouse 11%
Wheat 7%
Vegetables, sweet corn, and melons 9%
All other crops 16%

manmade

arts

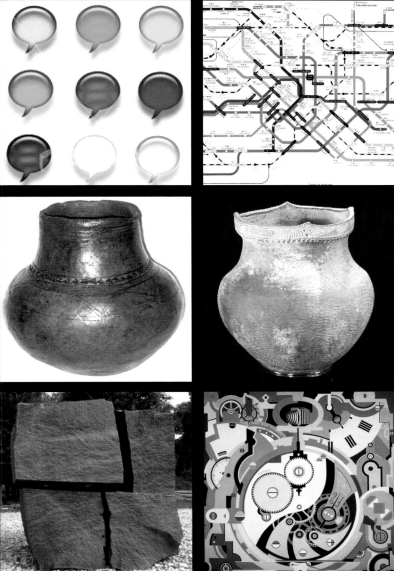

Shape

SHAPE investigations
to do on your own:

1. Explore your home as though it were a museum. What kinds of shapes have you collected, consciously or unconsciously? Make an arrangement of disparate objects that share a shapely characteristic on a bookshelf or windowsill. What would the catalog of these shapes say about you?

2. As you drive through your neighborhood, notice the shapes of buildings, homes, stores and other structures. Do the shapes that you see serve as clues to architectural eras, the history of the street? If yours is a new neighborhood, what historical styles have the builders called upon for inspiration? Shapes of windows, doors, rooflines and facades are your best clues.

3. Cut or tear shapes from colored paper and collage them to solid colored cards for interesting personal note paper.

4. Think about how your clothing affects your silhouette as you dress for work or play. Make an effort to wear something that changes your shape, and pay attention to its effect.

5. Collect a specific shape (circles or cones, for example) or specifically shaped objects (manholes, terracotta vases, interesting doors) by photographing throughout a day, a week, a month. Post your collection on a photography website, such as Flickr, to share it with others.

6. Take a walk along a creek bed or river and visually collect the shapes you see in stones and water.

7. Write a haiku each morning for a week about the weather outside your window. (How do constraints of syllable count shape your thoughts?)

SHAPE investigations
for you and your child:

1. Make a shape visit to the zoo, discussing the categories of shapes you find for particular animal parts: noses, ears, horns and antlers, feet and silhouettes.

2. Carry a couple of small cans of play clay with you on car rides or during waiting times in restaurants and offices. Challenge your child to sculpt shapes that communicate different moods and feelings.

3. Make cookies and cut them out with a collection of cookie cutters.

4. Sew a tube of stretch knit fabric large enough for your child to climb into and explore the shapes his or her body can make, pushing and pulling on the fabric — great for a homegrown monster movie.

5. Show your child how to fold and cut paper snowflakes or *papel picado* flags to decorate windows or a room for a festive meal.

6. Make a leaf collection: press your leaves in a discarded telephone directory, then, when dry, use them for stencils, leaf prints and scrapbooks.

7. Use a copier to make a booklet of simple shapes drawn by your child (circles, squares or triangles for youngest kids, more complex shapes for older ones). They finish each shape by completing it as a drawing of a different object or scene.

8. Take up ornithology, botany or another categorical field study with your child. The library or bookstore has plenty of resources and field guides that are targeted for beginners of any age. Any study of this kind builds shape recognition and distinction as you learn.

Talking About Shape:

The sky is round, and...the earth is round like a ball, and so are all the stars. The wind, in its greatest power, whirls. Birds make their nests in circles, for theirs is the same religion as ours. The sun comes forth and goes down again in a circle. The moon does the same and both are round. Even the seasons form a great circle in their changing, and always come back to where they were. The life of a man is a circle from childhood to childhood, and so it is in everything where power moves.

— Black Elk

The square is not a subconscious form. It is the creation of intuitive reason. It is the face of the new art. The square is a living, royal infant. It is the first step of pure creation in art. Before it, there were naïve deformities and copies of nature. Our world of art has become new, nonobjective, pure.

— Kasimir Malevich

Philosophy is written in this grand book—I mean the universe—which stands continually open to our gaze, but it cannot be understood unless one first learns to comprehend the language and interpret the characters in which it is written. It is written in the language of mathematics, and its characters are triangles, circles, and other geometrical figures, without which it is humanly impossible to understand a single word of it.

— Galileo Galilei

I said to myself, I have things in my head that are not like what anyone has taught me - shapes and ideas so near to me - so natural to my way of being and thinking that it hasn't occurred to me to put them down. I decided to start anew, to strip away what I had been taught.

— Georgia O'Keeffe

Sound

Sound words:
Ding, slurp, frizz, fizz, zipper, plop, ping,
grrrr, growl, sing, slap, clap, clang,
dingle, chime, chant, choir, roar, tone,
note, chord, loud, soft, vibrato, staccato,
mezzo, soprano, alto, bass, guitar, viola,
synthesizer, moog, midrange, screech,
slur, symphonic, whisper, shout, speak,
laugh, cough, blip, bling, blabber, jab-
ber, trill, splat, silent, sing, crash, clank,
gulp, click, tsk, hmmm, um, sigh, puff,
patter, humph, hum

everyday

nature

architecture

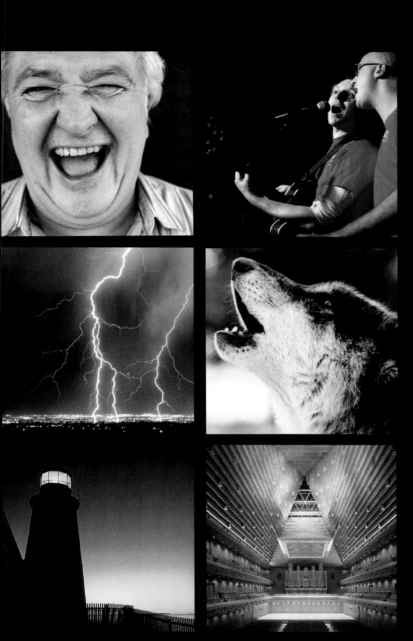

Sound

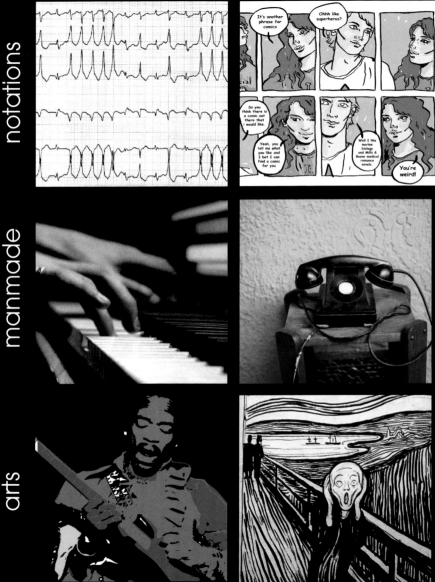

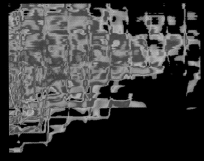

Sound

SOUND investigations
to do on your own:

1. Visit a natural setting and sit quietly. Make a list of all the sounds you hear in ten minutes. Imagine that you are from an alien planet, how would you characterize the sounds, what would they be "saying"?

2. Do the preceding exercise in a busy urban street, on a playground, in a retail store, inside your home. Compare and contrast.

3. Visit a record store or an on-line music store where you can listen to a wide variety of music. Take an auditory trip into realms you've never visited, whether they be urban hip-hop, trance electronica, Japanese pop, 12th century chant, etc. Open your ears.

4. Working from a theme, download a collection of music that fits a mood, a topic, a color.

5. Visit a variety of religious services, noting how sound and silence are used in different rituals.

6. Listen to a piece of vocal music and, using a pencil, notate and discover the underlying structure of chorus, musical bridges and narrative.

7. Hear the sounds of space (lightning on Saturn, Voyager Termination shock, sounds of the magnetosphere) at this website: http://www-pw.physics.uiowa.edu/space-audio/.

SOUND investigations
for you and your child:

1. Make up a kitchen pan band with your child and some friends. Play along with music, then make up your own. (okay, use earplugs, if you must!)

2. Collect sounds in the neighborhood, at a ballgame, in the park with a tape recorder.

3. Explore the use of a simple music composition software, such as Garageband.

4. How many sounds can the two of you make just using your body. Rude sounds allowed.

5. Make a sound mobile with recycled "beautiful trash." Hang it where you can hear the wind play music throughout the day.

6. Make a bottle, jar and water harmonica.

7. Make an ongoing collection of interesting simple instruments (great for travel momentos) – harmonicas, rattles, drums, shakers, whistles. Use them for performances with family and friends.

8. Make a collection of shakers and rattles using different containers and different items inside (for example empty plastic vitamin bottles filled with rice, sand, beans, beads, marbles.) Describe and distinguish the difference in sound.

Talking About Sound:

I will speak to you in stone-language
(Answer with a green syllable)
I will speak to you in snow-language
(Answer with a fan of bees)
I will speak to you in water-language
(Answer with a canoe of lightning)
I will speak to you in blood language
(Answer with a tower of birds)

— Octavio Paz

For most of us, it's revolutionary to find out that listening to or making music is not just for fun or to make you smarter, but can make you better at what you do. The systems that are enhanced by music seem to be endless.

— Eric Jensen

Music is the effort we make to explain to ourselves how our brains work. We listen to Bach transfixed because this is listening to a human mind.

— Lewis Thomas

My personal hobbies are reading, listening to music, and silence.

— Edith Sitwell

If you develop an ear for sounds that are musical it is like developing an ego. You begin to refuse sounds that are not musical and that way cut yourself off from a good deal of experience.

— John Cage

If you stand still outside you can hear it...winter's footsteps, the sound of falling leaves

— Takayuki Ikkaku

texture

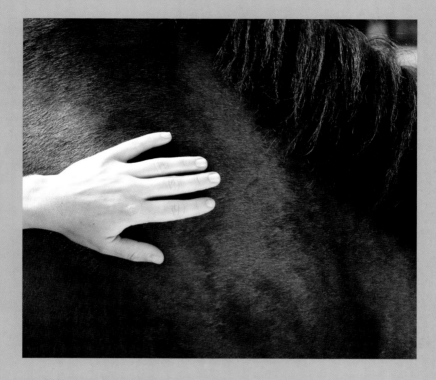

Texture words:
Smooooth, scratchy, glassy, shiny,
cracked, plaid, polkadots, ribbed, wiry,
dog's ear, curly, wavy, oily, fuzzy, hairy,
silky, ashy, prickly, woven, wet, wooly,
slick, melting, layered, soft, glossy,
doughy, puffy, bumpy, touch, ssslimy,
cool, chewy, tender, velvety

everyday

nature

architecture

Texture

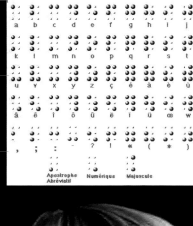

Apostrophe
Abréviatif | Numérique | Majuscule

Texture

TEXTURE investigations to do on your own:

1. Examine your wardrobe and make a texture inventory. What textures really suit you? What feels good against your skin? Make a point to buy something with a pleasing texture the next time you shop.

2. Cook a meal with a conscious plan to include contrasting textures, as the Japanese do. Do certain kinds of tastes correspond to certain kinds of textures? Think temperature as well as crisp, creamy, grainy, smooth.

3. Where can you experience coarse, slimy, mushy, matted, abrasive, elastic, sleazy, itchy, silky, downy, frothy, fuzzy? Consciously create one new tactile experience each day for a week.

4. Listen to different music with an ear toward texture: contemporary jazz, baroque, chant and heavy metal are a few contrasting genres to try.

5. Visit a museum's textile or fiber arts exhibitions or explore some online exhibitions or galleries. Try one or more of these key words for a search: fashion, art quilts, traditional quilts, art cloth, knitting, weaving, wearable art, basketry, fiber arts, shibori, batik.

6. Study and write a poem about the textures of your body, inside and out.

TEXTURE investigations
for you and your child:

1. Take a walk with a roll of tracing paper and large crayons or oil pastels. Make texture rubbings of grates, sidewalk surfaces, brick walls and other environmental elements.

2. Make a scrap box of textures – fabrics, paper, packaging materials, string, etc – and make texture cards, pictures and other art together.

3. Translate a piece of your child's art into a design for a quilt or wall hanging or pillow. Let your child help select the fabrics and textures. You can use iron-on bonding web to make the assembly fast and easy.

4. Garden together. Talk about the textures you feel as you work.

5. Talk about moods and behaviors in terms of texture: "Are you feeling itchy and scratchy – you can't seem to stop fidgeting – what would make you feel smooth and creamy?" Ask your child to describe your moods and actions as textures, too.

6. Play with textures of food and eating. What feels good in the mouth: mashed potatoes, corn on the cob, snow cones, chocolate? What feels not so good: chalky pills, string beans, okra? What else? Make an inventory.

7. Make a collection of drawings of the textures of all the neighborhood dogs' fur. (Or cats.)

Talking About Texture

Has anybody said publicly how nice it is to write on rubber with a ballpoint pen? The slow, fat, ink-rich line rolled over a surface at once dense and yielding, makes for a multidimensional experience no single sheet of paper can offer.

— Nicolson Baker

How swiftly the strained honey of afternoon light flows into darkness.

— *Lisel Mueller*

Indifference is isolation. In difference is texture and wonder.

— Edwin Schlossberg

Experience has taught me, when I am shaving of a morning, to keep watch over my thoughts, because, if a line of poetry strays into my memory, my skin bristles so that the razor ceases to act. The seat of this sensation is the pit of the stomach.

— *A.E. Housman*

Moisture and color and odor thicken here. The hours of daylight gather atmosphere.

— Robert Frost

The verbal poetical texture of Shakespeare is the greatest the world has known, and is immensely superior to the structure of his plays as plays. With Shakespeare it is the metaphor that is the thing, not the play.

— *Vladimir Nabokov*

Light

Light words: dark, bright, sparkle, glittery, gloom, sunrise, sunset, twilight, dingy, brilliant, dim, laser, metallic, sizzling, contrast, shadowy, shimmery, foggy, muted, translucent, transparent, opaque, glint, gleam, blinding, incandescent, florescent, halogen, ambient, spotlight, stark, floodlight, sun, reflection, irridescent, flash, star, moon, visibility, shaded, radiate, pinpoint

everyday

nature

architecture

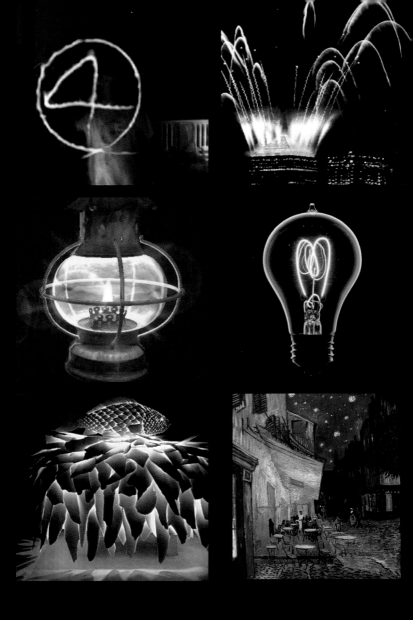

Light

LIGHT investigations
to do on your own:

1. Watch a classic black and white film on video or at a revival movie theater. How do the director and cinematographer use light as a language of expression? Compare the film to that of another director or a color film.

2. Take a black and white photography class and learn to develop and print your own film.

3. Make and use a pin-hole camera from instructions in a book or on the web, one site is www.pinhole.org. Use it to make unique photos of your environment.

4. Collect neon signs, especially those that speak of an earlier era of commerce or entertainment, by sketching or photographing their messages in light.

5. Notice the interplay of light and dark, shadow and sun along the road as you drive along a stretch of highway. If this is a route you take often, catalog the differences that the time of year and time of day make in your observations.

LIGHT investigations
to do with your child:

1. Plant several beans in soil-filled paper cups. Place them in different light conditions, provide the same amount of water each day, and make a chart to record growth and health.

2. Make solar prints with photosensitive paper available from toy stores or museum shops. Or experiment with solar art using Pebeo Transparent Paints on fabric squares, mixed and prepared according to the directions that come with the paint.

3. Play with hand shadows to create animals, people and shapes.

4. Fill interesting bottles and jars with colored water and line them up on a windowsill.

5. Play with form, light and shadow using a copy machine with objects such as rocks, shells, glass bottles, beads, your hands, black felt and white silk. Use the copier as if it were a black and white camera.

6. When it is time to change moods, behaviors or activity, signal the change in your home with a new light level, intensity or quality of light. Consciously use light as a cue for your child for waking, sleeping, resting, dining and other activities. Flick the lights as in a theater as a way to get attention! Dim the lights when it's time to settle down.

Talking About Light:

She has always been there, my darling.
She is, in fact, exquisite.
Fireworks in the dull middle of February
and as real as a cast-iron pot.

— Anne Sexton

All the means of action - the shapeless masses - the materials - lie everywhere about us. What we need is the celestial fire to change the flint into the transparent crystal, bright and clear. That fire is genius.

— *Henry Wadsworth Longfellow*

Awareness of the stars and their light pervades the Koran, which reflects the brightness of the heavenly bodies in many verses. The blossoming of mathematics and astronomy was a natural consequence of this awareness.

— Fatima Mernissi

Most people would guess that the sun is fifty or a hundred times brighter than the moon, but it's a half million times brighter – evidence of the amazing capacity of our eyes to adjust to light and dark.

— *James Elkins*

Moonlight is sculpture.

— Nathaniel Hawthorne

And light has no weight,
Yet one is lifted on its flood,
Swept high,
Running up white-golden light-shafts,
As if one were as weightless as light itself —
All gold and white and light.

—*Lawren Harris*

Movement

MOVEMENT words:
Run, gallop, slink, slither, kick, stick, lunge, loop, zip, zoom, clench, tackle, leap, dance, slump, stretch, gesture, grimace, evaporate, condense, retreat, retire, race, shuffle, slide, swing, swim, stitch, stir, dig, dip, dangle, twitch, turn, tug, tether, twist, spiral, spin, cast, catch, waltz, tango, polka, poke, pry, punch, float, fling, reach, rip, stir, slice, slop, slip

everyday

nature

architecture

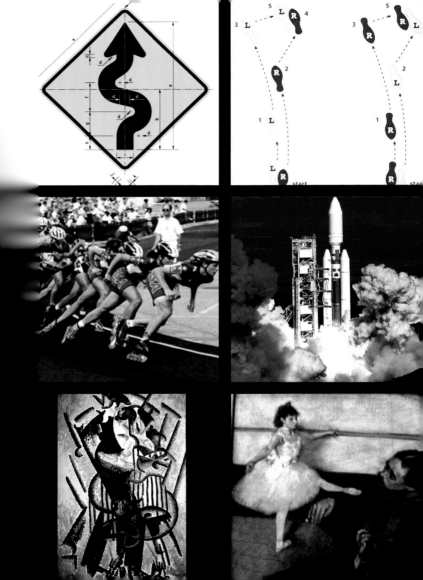

RTH ATLANTIC TROPICAL STORMS AND HURRICANES, 1851-2004 (

Movement

MOVEMENT investigations
to do on your own:

1. Learn to weave, knit or crochet. What does this kind of hand movement create in you?

2. Use a calligraphy brush or pen and sheets of smooth paper to experience different kinds of movement of your hand and wrist.

3. Move to a favorite piece of music. Then move to a style of music that's not on your playlist.

4. Wear a long skirt, a cape, a long coat or another kind of garment that changes the way you move. Pay attention.

5. Watch the movement of wind in trees and upon water. Try to capture the movement with sketches or photography.

6. Move, then draw or write about the images that popped into your head.

7. Photograph moving objects, animals, people and places with an intentionally slow shutter speed to catch interesting blurring evidence of movement. Or with a video camera, experiment with slow motion or speeded up playback.

MOVEMENT investigations
for you and your child:

1. Visit a roller skating rink or ice rink, even if you have to cling to the walls!

2. Accompany your child to a modern dance or folk dance performance. Play ball with different sizes and weights of bouncing balls.

3. Visit as many fountains as possible. Construct a tabletop or garden fountain for your home.

4. Hike, bike or rock climb. Record your movements afterwards with drawing and writing about the experience in a story you and your child write together.

5. Visit a carnival and discuss and compare the sensations of movement on different kinds of rides.

6. Teach your child some traditional jump rope chants. Join in.

7. Invent funny shoes to wear around the house—decorate house slippers, socks or clogs with colorful add-ons.

8. Build tin can stilts for a walk around the block together.

9. Make a homemade track with 1x2 wood strips and blocks for toy cars and other wheeled toys.

10. Let your child take apart something mechanical (and now broken) to see how it worked. Cut off any electric cords for safety's sake.

Talking About Movement:

There is a vitality, a life-force, an energy, a quickening that is translated through you into action and because there is only one of you in all of time, this expression is unique. And if you block it, it will never exist through any other medium and be lost.

— Martha Graham

Amazingly, the part of the brain that processes movement is the same part of the brain that's processing learning.

— Eric Jenson

Sometimes you get a glimpse of a semicolon coming, a few lines farther on, and it is like climbing a steep path through woods and seeing a wooden bench just at a bend in the road ahead, a place where you can expect to sit for a moment, catching your breath.

— Lewis Thomas

The dance is a poem of which each movement is a word.

— Mata Hari

My writing is like a ten gallon spring. It can issue from the ground anywhere at all. On smooth ground it rushes swiftly on and covers a thousand *li* in a single day without difficulty. When it twists and turns among mountains and rocks, it fits its form to things it meets: unknowable. What can be known is, it always goes where it must go, always stops where it cannot help stopping – nothing else. More than that, even I cannot know.

— Su Shih

Space

Space words:
tight, expansive, fluid, cosmic, random, arc,
loose, stage, stadium, arch, atrium, planet,
negative, positive, platform, plateau, up,
down, over, under, around, inner, outer, sky,
manmade, landlocked, understory, roadway,
cathedral, bridge, page, canvas, room,
undefined

everyday

nature

architecture

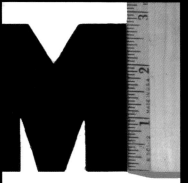

Space

SPACE investigations
on your own:

1. Rearrange the objects on one shelf or tabletop in your home or office, making thoughtful decisions about spatial relationships.

2. Investigate the Japanese philosophy and practice of feng shui. Try putting one or more of the principles in action in your home or office and see if you notice a difference.

3. Imagine your day as a map. Draw it.

4. Visit several sacred and/or public buildings that have very different spatial characteristics – for example, a large church sanctuary, the lobby of a busy corporation, a transportation hub, such as a bus terminal or airport lobby, a historical chapel or synagogue? Journal about how each of the spaces made you feel, move and think.

5. Read a book or watch a video about quantum theory or string theory (www.ted.com>tedtalks).

6. Spend a day intentionally standing closer to others when you speak to them. What happens to your sense of personal space?

SPACE investigations
for you and your child:

1. Design towns and communities with blocks, sand or clay, even a collection of recyclable boxes, cans, and cardboard tubes. Imagine together what the city of the future might be like.

2. Help your child fill a shoebox with items that tell about him or her and put it away for a year as a short-term time capsule. Include a photo, a height and weight record, a list of favorites and small treasures. Make the filling of the box part of the process, designing compartments, pages that turn, pop-up elements, etc.

3. Use sheets and blankets over furniture to make indoor tents and tunnels.

4. Find as many one-mile walks from and back to your front door as are possible in your neighborhood.

5. With young children, play with volume and shape by pouring rice or water or sand from one shaped container to another.

6. Visit a children's museum together and talk about how the designers created interesting spaces and spatial relationships.

Talking About Space:

The space within becomes the reality of the building.
— Frank Lloyd Wright

That great Cathedral space which was childhood.
— Virginia Woolf

To me every hour of the light and dark is a miracle. Every cubic inch of space is a miracle.
— Walt Whitman

Space is to place as eternity is to time.
— Joseph Joubert

Space is big. You just won't believe how vastly, hugely, mind-bogglingly big it is. I mean, you may think it's a long way down the road to the drug store, but that's just peanuts to space.
— Douglas Adams

Music was my refuge. I could crawl into the space be-
tween the notes and curl my back to loneliness.
— Maya Angelou

Darkness is to space what silence is to sound, i.e., the interval.
— Marshall Mcluhan

What art offers is space - a certain breathing room for
the spirit.
—John Updike

Space and light and order. Those are the things that men need just as much as they need bread or a place to sleep.
— Le Corbusier

Rhythm

Some rhythm words: walk, run, gallop, jump, saunter, skip, stomp, swing, meander, undulate, leap, sneak, hiccup, yawn, giggle, yap, blink, gossip, chatter, tiptoe, doze, beat, tempo, time, staccato, adagio, largo, allegro, nervous, jittery, busy, calm, slow, antics, habit, routine, ritual, rut, holiday, celebration, rhumba, waltz, tango, hip-hop, march, rock'n roll

Rhythm

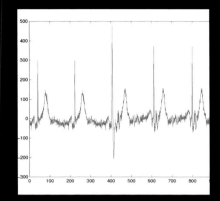

This is my

Working Rhythm
ChARLie

Rhythm

RYHTHM investigations
to do on your own:

1. From your collection of CDs, choose three different genres of music that use rhythm in a distinct way (for example, tango, country swing, Gregorian chant). Using a large pad of paper and a marker or charcoal, draw lines as you listen to each kind of music.

2. Read a favorite author aloud. Consider his or her use of rhythm. Try this with a few other writers of different genres of literature – poetry, essay, fiction – even advertising copy.

3. Notice the sonic rhythms of these kinds of objects: an expressway during rush hour, sailboats on a lake, cicadas or tree frogs at night, the laugh track of a TV sitcom. If you can, tape record one or more of these sounds and then speed up and slow down the tape to find out more about the rhythm.

4. Make a collection of rhythm photographs from a walk through your neighborhood. Shoot photos at morning, noon and night.

5. Think about and write a page or two about a person whom you know well (should be someone past age 18, whose personal rhythm is well defined). Clap out his or her rhythm (don't think too hard about this one); then "perform" the rhythm for another person. Ask your audience to tell you what kind of person you are describing in rhythm. See what communicates.

6. Visit a place that you think has a peaceful tranquil meditative rhythm. Sit quietly for 20 minutes and see what happens to your state of mind.

7. Take twice as much time to eat breakfast as you usually do. Dress in half the time (or twice the time). How does rhythm affect your routines?

RHYTHM investigations
for you and your child:

1. Turn a game of catch into a rhythm game by consciously varying the pace and placement of a bounced beach ball, tennis ball or foam ball.

2. Take a rhythm walk around the block or around the playground: follow the leader with different rhythms to your walk. With older children, take your cue from the people you see on your walk.

3. Look for music that matches tasks you and your child can do together (a march, 50s rock and roll, gospel or klezmer, operatic overture or swing). Talk about whether a certain kind of musical rhythm makes the job easier or more fun.

4. Next time you ask your child to do something, ask using a different rhythm than the one you usually use for such requests.

5. Make a collection of rhythms from family lore with your child: the counting rhymes your parents knew, jump rope, hand-clap and other game chants, even jokes that rely on rhythm like knock-knock jokes.

6. The next time your child has a memorization task (for example—learning the multiplication tables) "warm up" with a rhythmic game using sound and movement.

Talking About Rhythm:

Almost all American white people at that time seemed to think that all Negroes could sing and dance and that all of us had a sense of rhythm. So I came to the conclusion that maybe poetry, rhythm, color, me a Negro, that little boy had thought he must have some rhythm to give a poem, and maybe that's why I was elected the class poet. Anyway I'm glad that I was.

— Langston Hughes

The drum is sacred. Its round form represents the whole universe, and its steady beat is the pulse, the heart, throbbing at the center of the universe.

—Nick Black Elk

A book is a part of life, a manifestation of life, just as much as a tree or a horse or a star. It obeys its own rhythms, its own laws, whether it be a novel, a play, or a diary. The deep, hidden rhythm of life is always there—that of the pulse, the heart beat.

— Henry Miller

When we experience a film, we consciously prime ourselves for illusion. Putting aside will and intellect, we make way for it in our imagination. The sequence of pictures plays directly on our feelings. Music works in the same fashion; I would say that there is no art form that has so much in common with film as music. Both affect our emotions directly, not via the intellect. And film is mainly rhythm; it is inhalation and exhalation in continuous sequence. Ever since childhood, music has been my great source of recreation and stimulation, and I often experience a film or play musically.

— Ingmar Bergman

Part 4:

Reflecting

Reflecting

The world is so full of a number of things,
I'm sure we should all be as happy as kings.

— Robert Louis Stevenson

Reflection — looking at the internal mirror of our thoughts and actions — is an important part of the creative process for all of us — parents, children and authors too. We see in our reflecting mind's eye a kaleidoscope of images, impressions, and data about the "metacognitive" (that layer that has to do with thinking about — witnessing — our own thinking).

Reflecting upon one's process always leads to unfolding paths — "what ifs," "what nexts," — to new entry points and new points of departure. As we reflect back over the material we've presented in this book, we hope we've made the case for the importance of the individual creative potential in children's lives today. We also hope to have given parents some basic tools and ideas for identifying and enhancing each child's special brand of creativity.

We've purposely avoided talking much about digital technology. What we want to address is the *thinking* behind the images and icons and sound and motion that pour out of the monitors and screens, not the screens themselves. It's kind of like saying that writing is about more than pencils.

Whether the tools you and your children use are as simple as clay and paste, or as advanced as digital cameras, CSS and podcasting, the creative content is more than the form it takes. Heading "back to the boards" is the way the choreographer Martha Graham described her creative necessity. And that also tells us we each must begin with our own individually unique perspective in order to create with power and fluency. All the fancy tools in the world do not make a great work of art or science, architecture or astronomy, literature or lunar exploration — the idea and passion always precede the technology.

This book describes a methodology for peeling back labels, rediscovering a more elemental way of viewing the world and ourselves, one that encourages describing but not defining, contrasting but not judging, curiosity instead of right answers. We advocate engaging the primary sensory data that can spawn many ways of knowing and many forms of expression.

Honing the observation skills that build sensory awareness drives attention deep into the world around us. As many seem more and more wed to exploration via the "virtual," this book is an argument for real life, real trips, "hands-on" real stuff. (It's the broadest bandwidth there is.)

The process of consciously making associations outside conventional boundaries can be an ongoing activity of daily life, one that is most effectively guided and modeled by parents. Putting the creative process into practice at home builds powerful thinking templates for children to follow.

To that end, this last chapter takes off with some up-close ideas and reminders for making room for creativity in the context of everyday:

New World Kids
FUNdamental Tips for Parents

1. IT'S WORTH IT!

It's worth the trouble and the time and the thinking and the mess! With the pressures on parents today to provide lessons, media gadgets and all the *stuff* guaranteed to help your child (and fill all her time), it can feel like you're going against the grain to protect open playtime and allow time for daydreams — even boredom. Finding a balance between structured learning and open space for imaginative play honors and extends your child's unique inventive potential and creates a priceless legacy.

2. BE A BIG MIRROR

A big part of nurturing your child's inventive potential is simply your own unspoken positive attitude and the willing support you provide to your child.

3. BACK TO THE FUTURE

Making deep and elemental connections with the real world through firsthand sensory information is one important key to building a strong, fluent and creative mind. In our post-modern time, this often means a return to the world *outside*, leaving behind the electronic boxes *inside* our homes. Cognitive tools for this firsthand exploration — observation, collection, communication through and with sight, smell, taste, sound, movement and touch — are the best equipment we can give kids for their future.

4. USE OPEN-ENDED STRUCTURES

Guiding a child's thinking is easier when parents whittle down the wide open world to create viewpoints for young eyes. Provide *focus* (e.g., ask your child to collect 20 different shapes of leaves, not merely to "look at trees and plants") — or specific problems to solve (make placecards for the Thanksgiving table with this paper, these pens and stickers).

5. POTENT PLAYTIMES
Active, imaginative play that children initiate has been proven by cognitive researchers to be deeply important to growing minds. "Playing like" and "pretending" are thinking in action and let children rehearse for real life without the worry of consequences.

6. BE FLEXIBLE
Use your *own* best ideas to design activities, spaces and materials to elicit your child's inventive thinking. This can be a messy process — it's always a bit experimental and may not produce the results you envision (and likely not what you would have done yourself). That's okay. What we do with our children as we engage their imaginations and creative thinking is far more about the *process* than the *product.*

7. FORGET COMPETITION
This is not a race. It is the opposite. Finding a child's special gifts and mirroring them back is what makes the "aha!" happen and creates the mental space for ideas. Finding your child's gifts is a process nurtured by parental "antennae," not by competition.

8. JOIN IN
Sometimes setting the scene, planning the trip, supplying the viewpoint or the materials then standing back to watch what unfolds is enough. Sometimes getting down on the floor, playing the game or sewing the specially designed dog's costume is essential. Join the fun when asked. This is memory making.

9. KEEP IT LIGHT

Keep the emphasis on playfulness — if children feel the weight of a parent's expectation, imagination is inhibited. Putting a child in the position of trying to please is not what it's about. Enjoy the surprises. Play detective.

10. ENLIST GRANDPARENTS

Get help. Grandparents, favorite uncles or other special adults are in a perfect position to help hold the big picture for your child. They don't have to worry about homework, soccer practice and carpools, after all. They might have time to play and can be great advocates for young creators. Bring them into the picture with ideas, plans, outings and events. They may even be waiting to be asked!

11. THINK DRAMA — USE SCALE

"Blowing up an idea" so that it can be seen is a good way to a underscore a child's imagination. For example, help your child make a real "play" and invite an audience, or cook and serve a special recipe invention to guests, or make a six-foot painting and feature it on the porch. Enlarging the scale helps kids see their ideas at work — and makes them important and memorable.

12. USE "SCRATCH" MATERIALS

Think about how many good things to eat can be made from scratch ingredients like flour, butter, eggs and cream! Apply those guidelines to the materials and toys you provide for your children. Many of today's toys demand a narrow range of responses from children, limiting their associative value. Recall the fun children have had for centuries with sticks, mud, rocks, sand, clay, wood scraps and string. Make sure these kinds of scratch materials are part of your child's playtimes.

13. TEMPER EXPECTATIONS

When your child is in the midst of a grand experiment of some kind, it's easy to get carried away and want to impose your own ideas and wishes, or think what *you* would do is what your child *should* do. Keep the "big picture" at the forefront of your mind and remember that children don't necessarily need a finished product to grow ideas.

14. EXPAND DEFINITIONS OF "INTERACTIVE"

Many toys and games advertise "interactivity" for the child, but often that means there are very few choices to make or play that is quite formulaic. The most valuable kind of "interactive" happened long before they even coined the word.

15. SEE KID CONCOCTIONS AS IMPORTANT INFORMATION

Closely observe the kinds of play your child comes up with on his own time — in a waiting room, when there's just a piece of paper and pen, with a buddy in the backyard or at the park. You'll be able to compile an ever more accurate profile of his individual strengths. Sometimes this is easier when you can also watch other children and note the differences. It's not about "better or worse" — and your child's strengths are bound to be different from your own strengths. Step back and collect this visual information as pure data to help you both refine and extend your *next* creative ideas for your child.

Finally, to close this book, we once more step back from the day-to-day path to take the long view:

We need all the children now.

We need the ones who are hard-wired for movement — they will become the dancers, athletes, coaches — the ones who have to move to think.

We need the ones who are especially sensitive to the vibrations and needs of other people and animals — they are the potential police officers, dramatists, vets, teachers, biologists, managers, psychologists, healers — the ones who have to feel to think.

We need the ones who naturally think in 3D — the future architects, surveyors, industrial designers, sculptors, homebuilders, urban planners, masons, engineers — the ones who need to experience space to think.

We need the ones who experience the world in images — the next photojournalists, graphic and web designers, filmmakers — the ones who think through their eyes.

We need the linear thinkers — the potential writers, storytellers, mathematicians, planners, draftsmen, logicians, playwrights, chemists — the ones who think best in linear arcs.

We need the ones who are innately attuned to the earth and its cycles — the budding botanists, cosmologists, farmers, astronomers, conservationists — the ones who naturally think in the larger patterns of our planet.

We need the ones who touch — the next weavers, chefs, physicians, carpenters, potters, gardeners — the ones who think with their hands.

We need the ones who innately recognize sonic power — the next composers, birders, musicians, singers, acoustic engineers — the ones who think in sound.

Please note: the careers listed come from a 20th century lexicon. They don't even scratch the surface of what lies just over the horizon in the immediate future. Currently, the "30,000-foot view" of our 21st century presents an awesome spectrum, one that spans large-scale and critical problems of global survival to amazing discoveries and possible solutions to those problems in diverse and overlapping fields of study.

Reflecting on this near future brings our children's educational needs into a sharper focus. As we noted in the introduction to this book, our schools — even the best of them — seem stuck in a pedagogy of the past. Assurance that our children can participate successfully in this time of unparalleled change and shifting boundaries of the future will require their best individual creative thinking.

The "back to basics" clarion call is of limited reach. It neither encompasses the myriad media in young lives nor provides the thinking tools for innovation that our children need now and tomorrow. At this time, parents are the literal keys to opening the doors of change.

We want our New World Kids to be confident of the gifts they bring into the world and confident in themselves as creators. Each of them embodies an absolutely unique perspective, and, collectively, they need the clear vision and the sure footing to carry us all into the next Renaissance.

The future needs all the children now.

Acknowledgements

We gratefully acknowledge the contributions made to this book and its philosophy from all the teachers, children and parents along the way throughout nearly a half century of creative exploration and experimentation.

The words you read here owe a debt of gratitude to all who were long ago part of Kitty Baker and Jearnine Wagner's Baylor Children's Theatre, the "mother ship" that gave birth to the Dallas Children's Theatre, the Unlimited Potential program and eventually, the Learning About Learning Educational Foundation.

Learning About Learning was the crucible for our research in creativity, our lab school, and our work in the San Antonio community and holds a special place in our hearts. We acknowledge the extraordinary gifts and work of our colleagues Dr. Cynthia Herbert, Julia Jarrell and Nancy Busch and also wish to thank the other staff members, donors, board members and participants who contributed to its influence as a national model and research institute for arts in education.

These ideas most recently found form at the Aldrich Contemporary Museum in Ridgefield, Connecticut. and we appreciate the far-sighted vision of Director, Harry Philbrick and Education Director, Nina Carlson for extending the idea of what museum education can be. The original New World Kids, pictured throughout this book, are: Ananya Amrithalingam, Catie Barrie, Grace Bucci, Will Forest, Pedro Lima, Isobel McCann, Lily Meyler, Henry Meyler, Helen Riser, Matteo Rubini, Niels Sogaard and Simon Van Wees. Our programmatic experiments with New World Kids helped us forge new territory and the images of the children enrich our words here.

It was Liener Temerlin and Stan Richards, the celebrated "admen" from Dallas, who first said, "it's time for this." Their encouragement along the way has inspired and enlivened this effort — and we thank them.

Thanks, too, to Cory Leahy (former LAL child) and Pam Losefsky for able and sensitive editing assistance. And, our dearest thank you's are for our partners, Richard Marcus and Linda Cuéllar — for their patience, support, encouragement and the many close and helpful readings during the time it took to produce this book.

For more information,
communication and downloads,
find us here:

www.newworldkids.org

Photographic Credits

Nina Carlson: cover
Allison V. Smith: pp 34,35,36,39
and from the Sensory Alphabet sections
(pp105-180):

1	2	3	4
5	6	7	8
9	10	11	12

(chart above indicates position)

Color A- 1,2,3,5,7,12
Line - cover
A- 1,2,3,4,5,7,10,11
Shape – cover
A- 1,2,3,4,5,6,8,10,12
Sound A- 1,2,3,4,6,
B- 6,8
Texture – cover
A- 1,2,3,4,5,8,
Light A-1,2,3,4,7,11
Movement – cover
A- 1,2,5,7,8
B- 7
Space – cover
A- 1,2,3,4,6,8
Rhythm – cover
A- 3,9,11,12

The balance of the photgraphs are from the collection of Susan Marcus.

Credit for Art

Sculpture on page 2 (with children):
David Abir | *Tecknar, Study Four* | 2004-2005

Credits for art work throughout the Sensory Alphabet chapter:

COLOR (112-113)
10. Unknown | *Head of Makakasyap*. Detail | 600-650 | Chinese | Kyzil. Turfan. China. | | ©Kathleen Cohen
11. Sonia Delauney-Terk | *Prismes Électriques* | 1914 | France. | | ©Kathleen Cohen
12. Paul Cezanne | *Apples & Oranges* | 1895-1900 | Paris. Musée d'Orsay. | | ©Kathleen Cohen

LINE (120-121)
9. Edgar Degas | *Four Dancers*. Detail. | c. 1899 | France. | | ©Kathleen Cohen
11. Grant Wood | *Haying* | 1939 | American | | ©Kathleen Cohen
12. Paul Gauguin | *Self-Portrait* | 1889 French | Washington D.C. National Gallery of Art. | | ©Kathleen Cohen

SHAPE (128-129)
10. Amedeo Modigliani | *Caryatid* | c. 1910-1920 | Italian | Paris. France. | | ©Kathleen Cohen
11. Izumi Masatoshi | *Fuyu* | 2008 | Japan
12. Gerald Murphy | *Watch* | 1888-1964 | American | Dallas Museum of Art, gift of the artist 1963

SOUND (136-137)
10. Edvard Munch | *The Scream* | 1895 | Norwegian | | ©Kathleen Cohen
11. Jules Breton | *The Song of the Lark* | 1884 | French | | ©Kathleen Cohen
12. Wassily Kandinsky | *Sounds* | Russian | Dallas Museum of Art, gift of Schatzie and George Lee, 2003

TEXTURE (144-145)
10. Paul Cezanne | *Self-Portrait* | 1883-1887 | French | | ©Kathleen Cohen
11. Vincent Van Gogh | *Sunflowers* | 1889 Dutch | Amsterdam. Rijksmuseum Vincent van Gogh | | ©Kathleen Cohen
12. Anonymous Early 16th c Flemish tapestry | *Wine making*. Detail | Paris. Musée National des Thermes | | ©Kathleen Cohen

LIGHT (152-153)
10. Vincent Van Gogh | *Outdoor Cafe; Starry Night* | 1888 | Dutch | Rijksmuseum Kroller-Muller | | ©Kathleen Cohen
12. Rembrandt van Rijn | *Anatomy Lesson of Nicholas Tulp* | 1632 | Dutch | Netherlands. The Hague | | ©Kathleen Cohen

MOVEMENT (160-161)
9. Gino Severini | *The Dance of the Bean at the Moulin Rouge* | 1913 | | ©Kathleen Cohen
10. Edgar Degas | *The Dance Lesson* | 1879 | French | | ©Kathleen Cohen
11. Paul Nash | *Battle of Britain* | 1941 | London Imperial War Museum | | ©Kathleen Cohen

SPACE (168-169)
9. Claude Monet | *Parliament at Sunset* | 1903 | French | | ©Kathleen Cohen
10. Pieter Jannsens | *Perspective Box* | 17 c | Netherlands | | ©Kathleen Cohen
11. (child sitting in...) David Abir | *Tecknar, Study Four* | 2004-2005
12. Juan Gris | *Portrait of Pablo Picasso* | 1912 | Spanish | | ©Kathleen Cohen

RHYTHM (176-177)
9. Kazimir Severinovic Malevich | *Aeroplane Flying* | 1915 | Russian | | ©Kathleen Cohen
10. Antoine-Louis Barye | *Elephant* | 19th c . | French | | ©Kathleen Cohen
11. Johnson William Henry | *Swing Low Sweet Chariot* | 1944 | American | | ©Kathleen Cohen
12. Hans Hoffman | *Untitled Landscape* | c. 1941 | American | | ©Kathleen Cohen

Special thanks to Kathleen Cohen for her permission to use the images from the World Image Project.